what is a home?

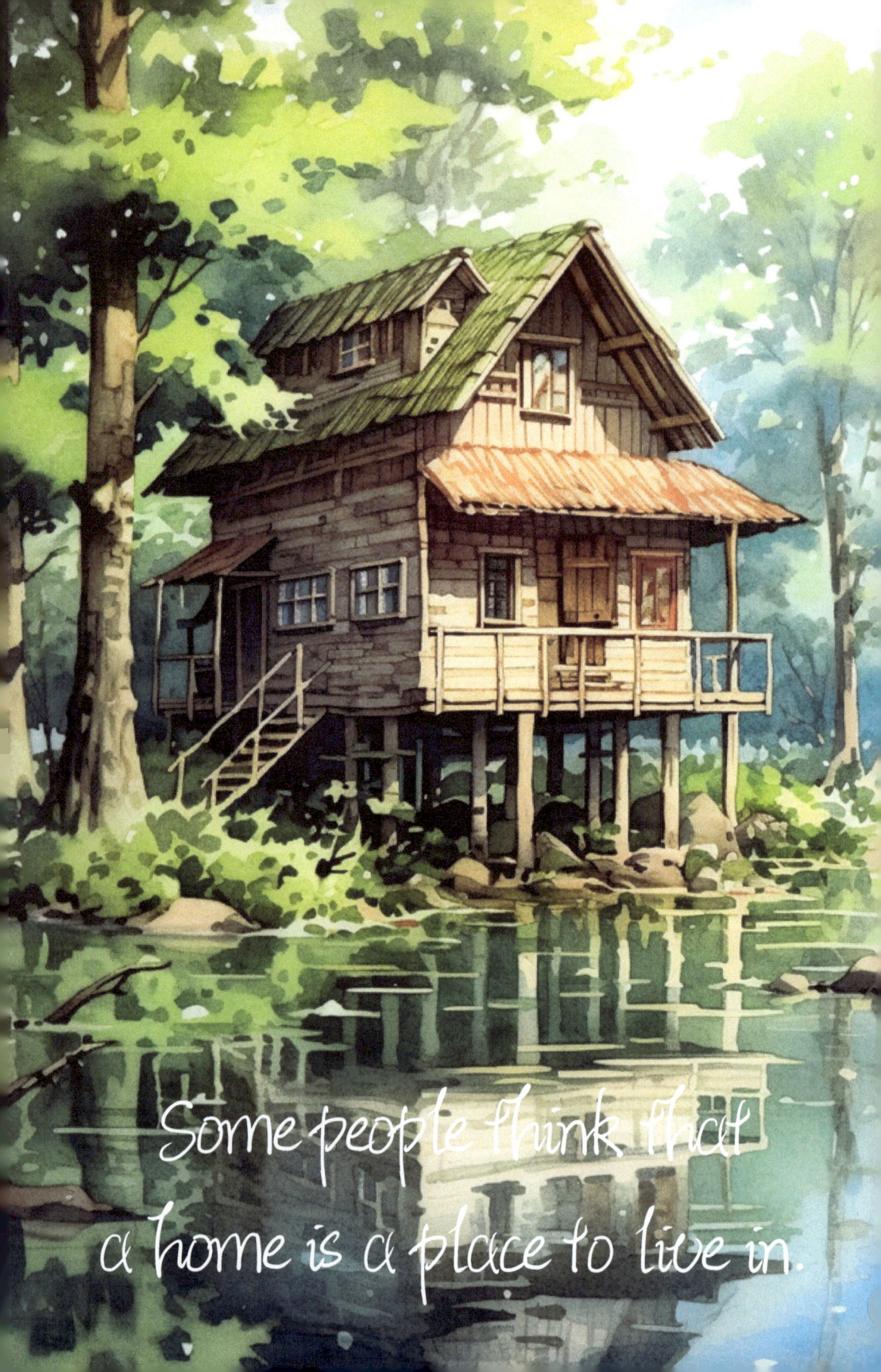

Some people think that a home is a place to live in.

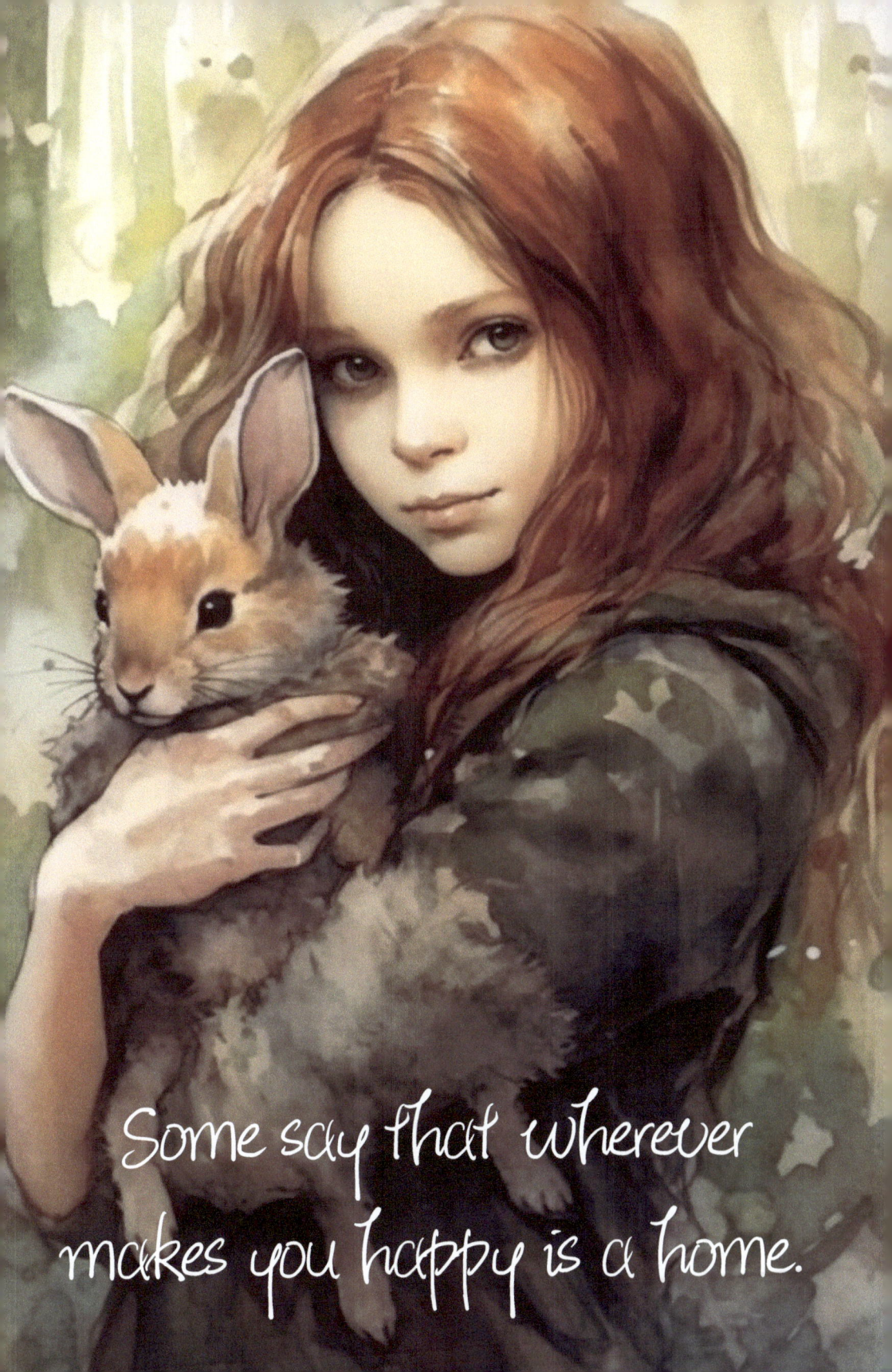

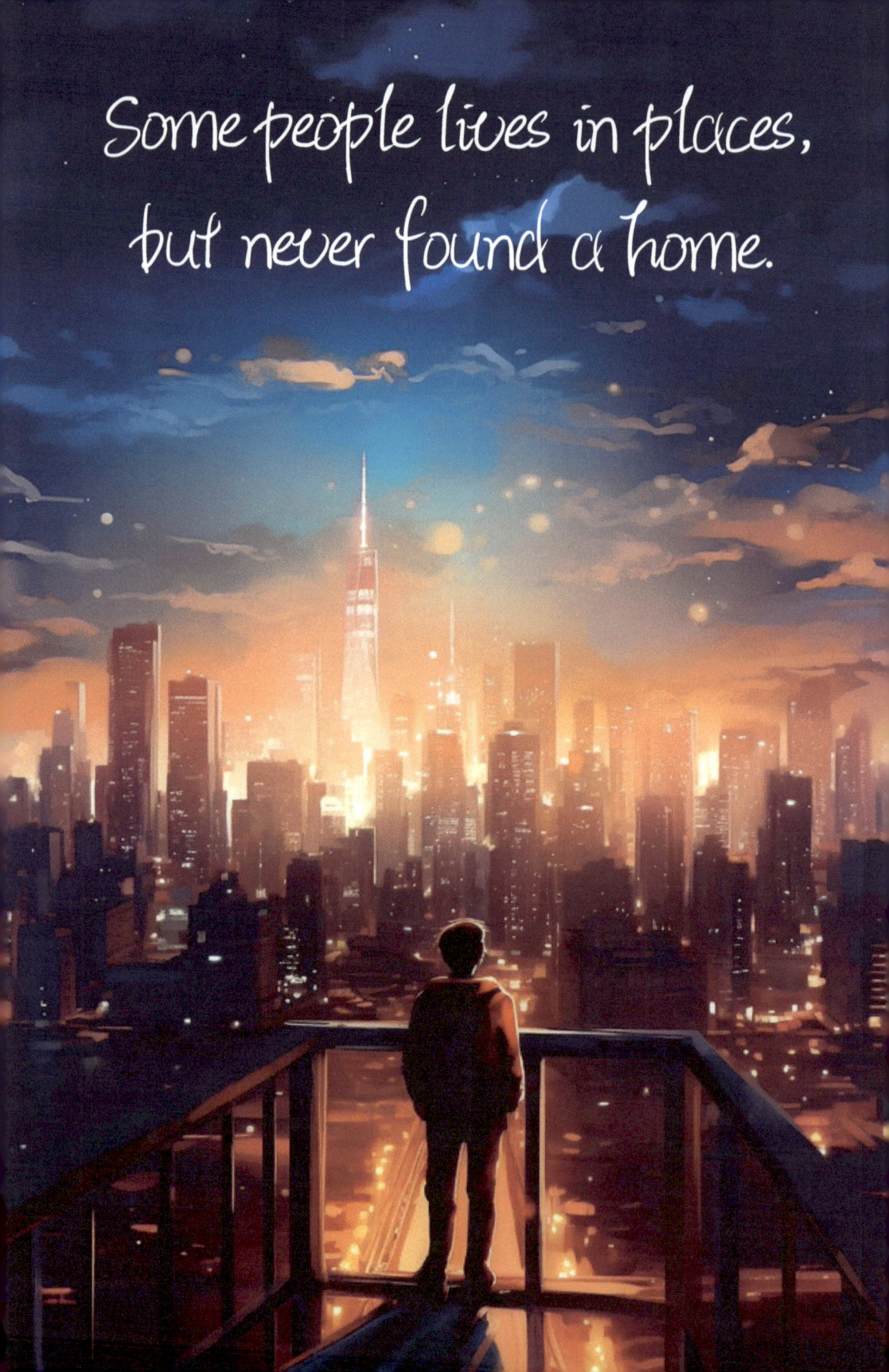

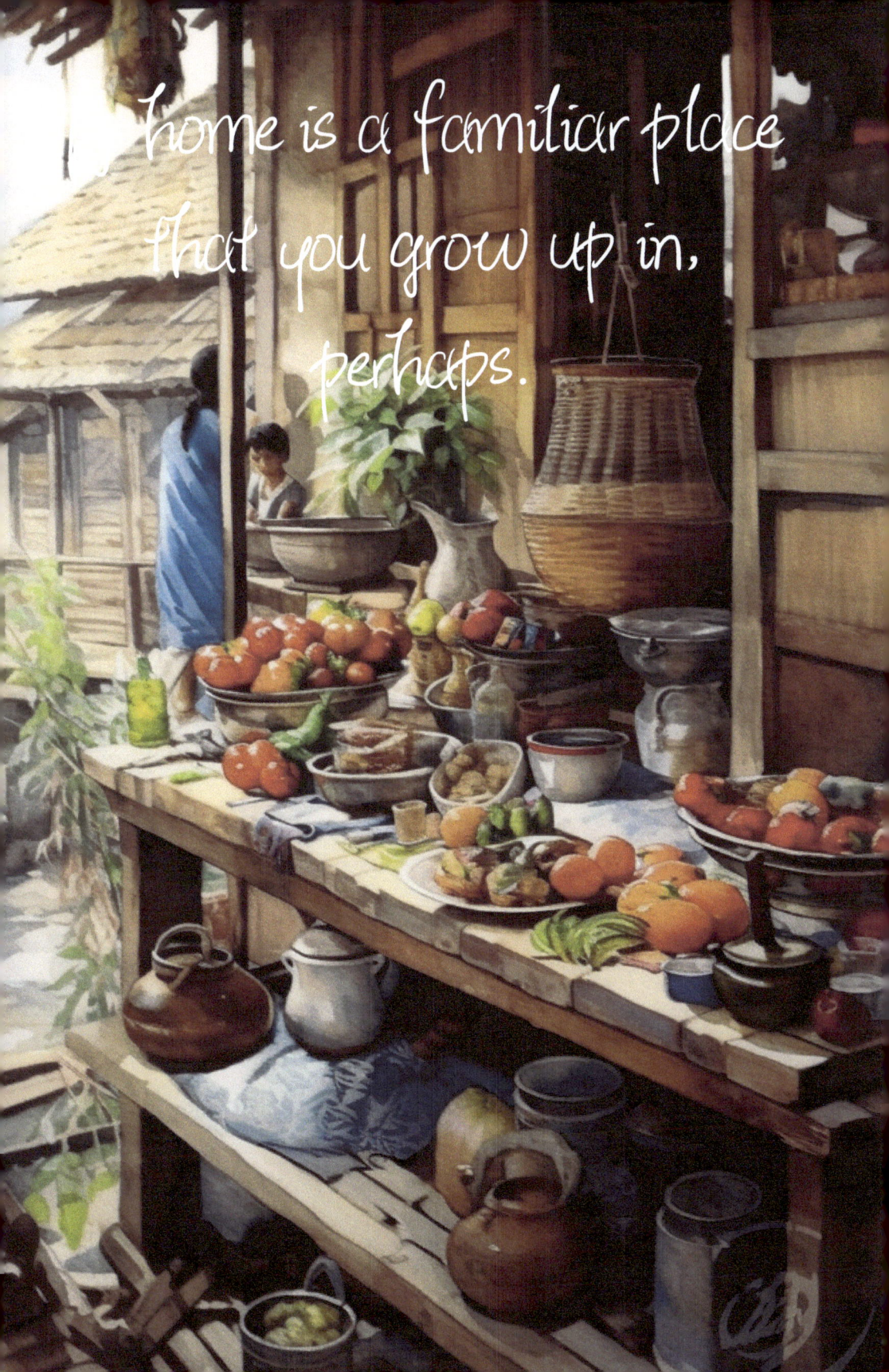

home is a familiar place that you grow up in, perhaps.

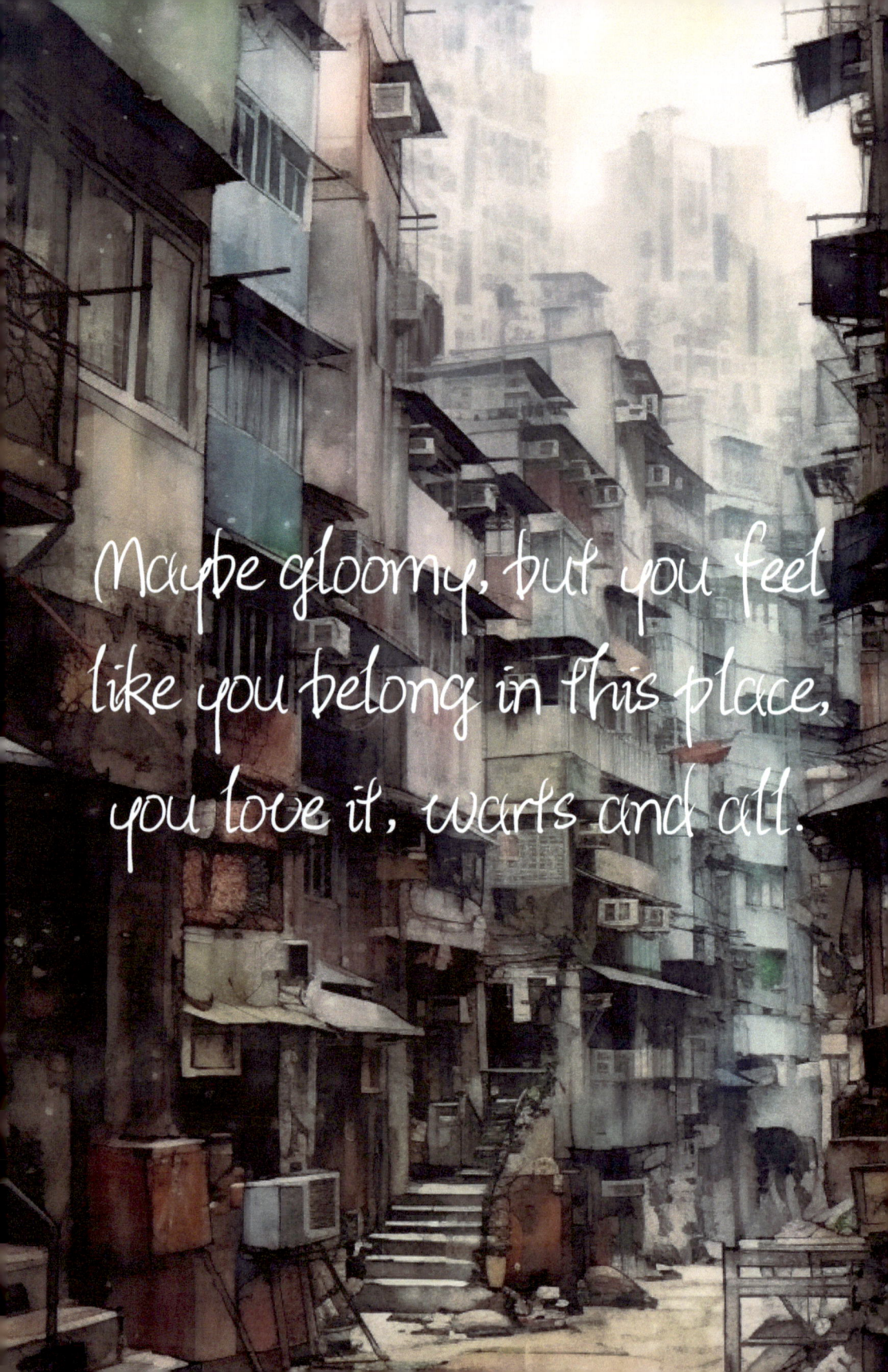

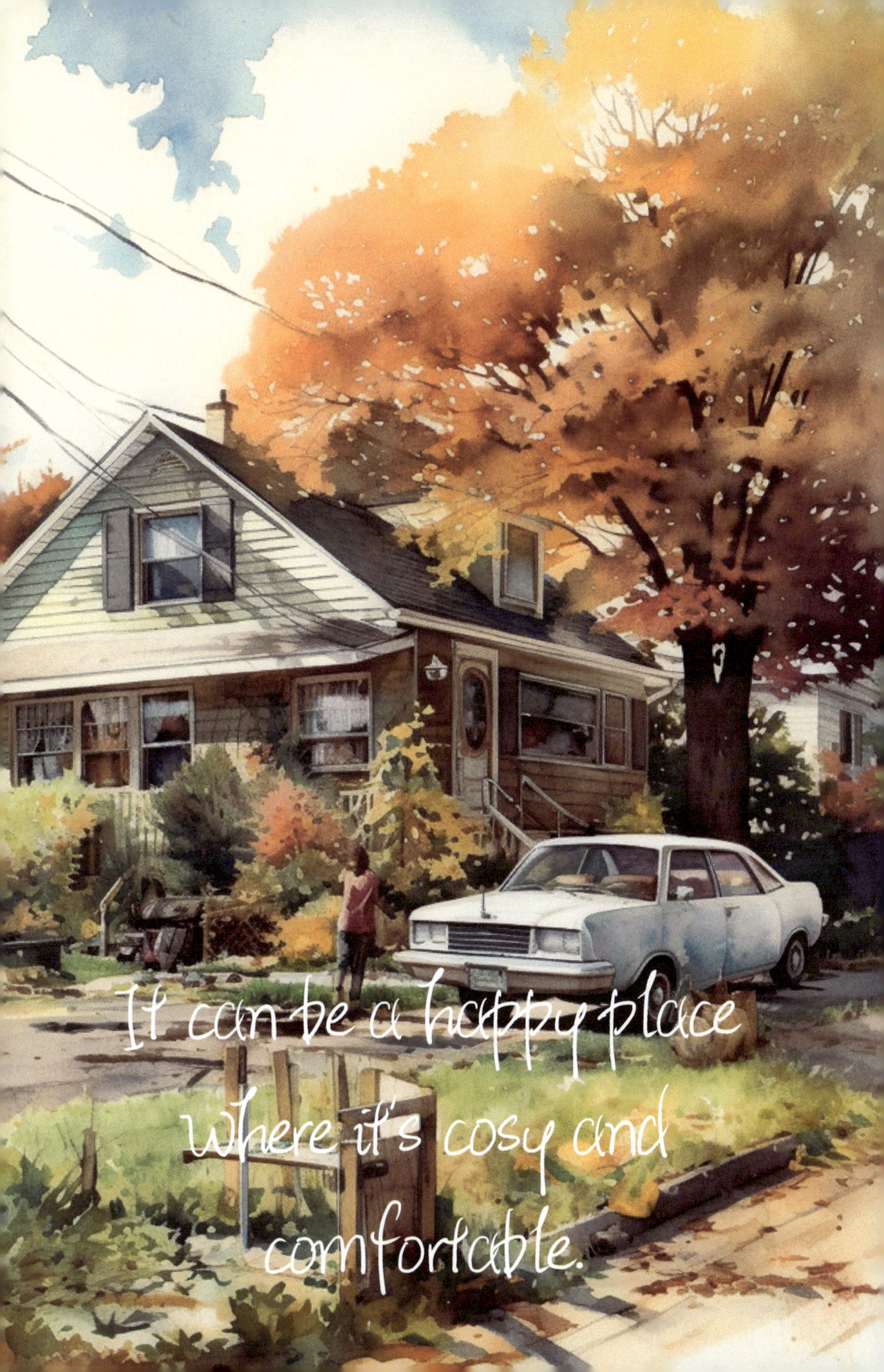

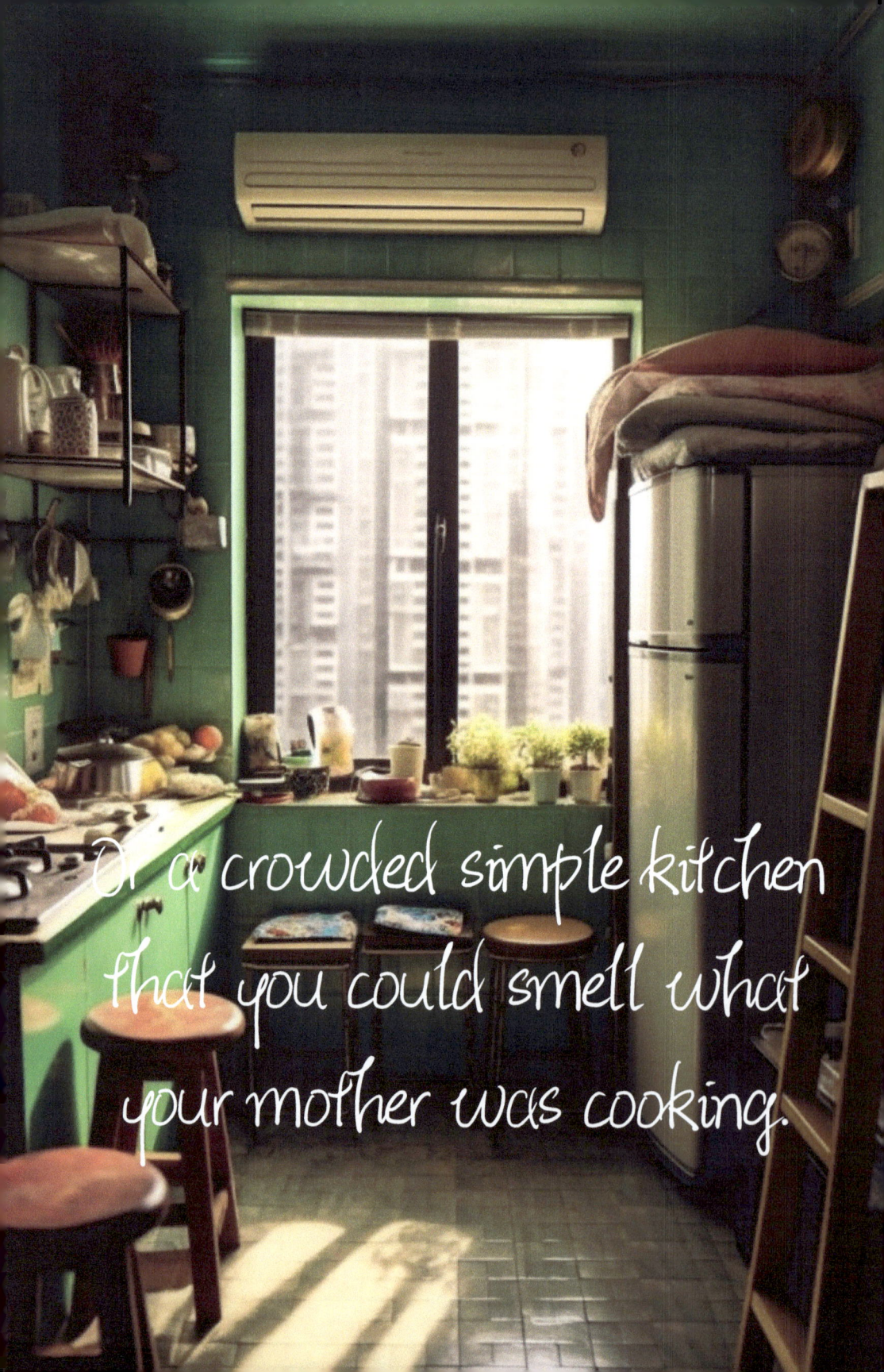
Or a crowded simple kitchen that you could smell what your mother was cooking.

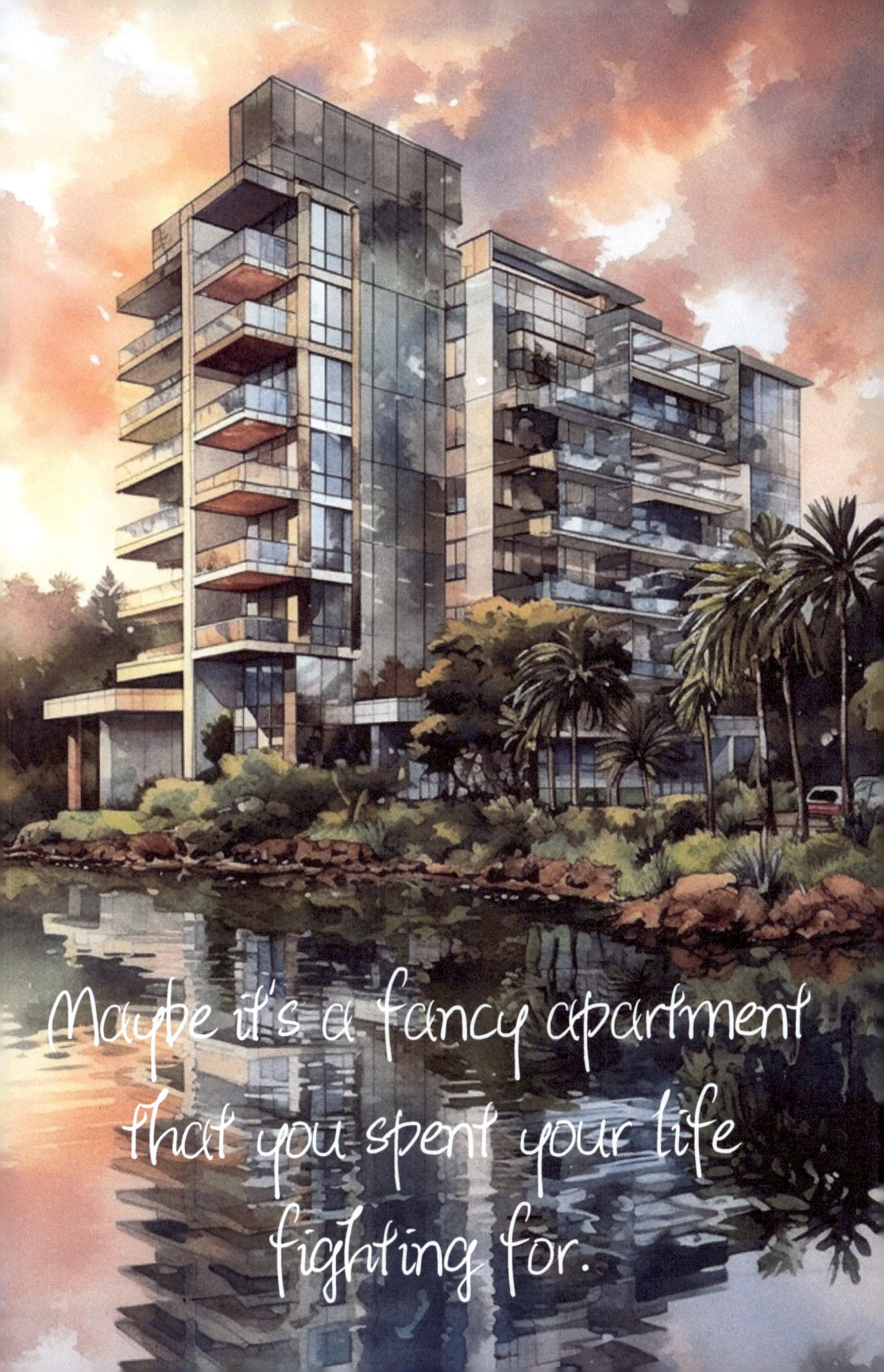

Maybe it's a fancy apartment that you spent your life fighting for.

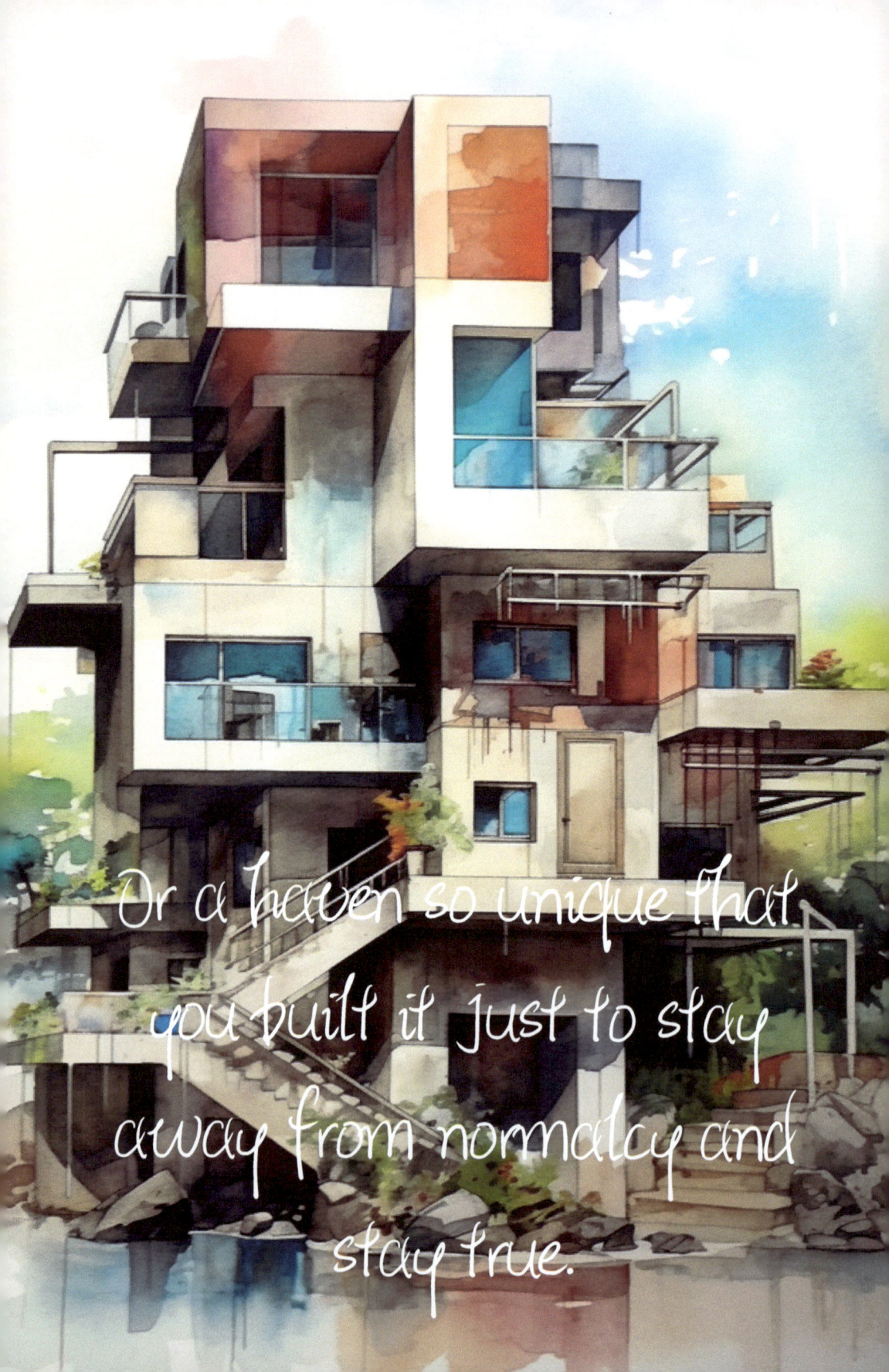

Or a haven so unique that you built it just to stay away from normalcy and stay true.

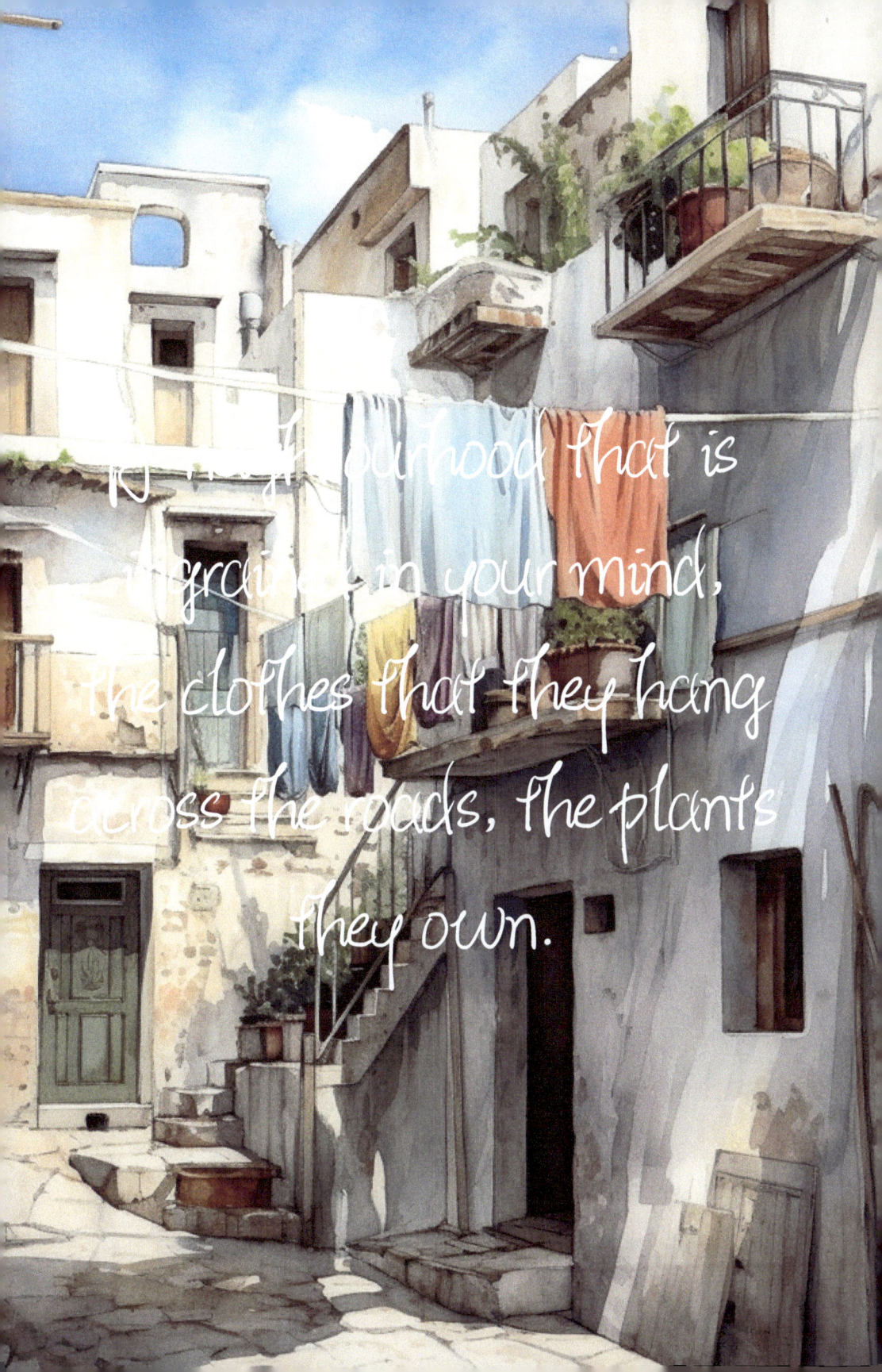

A neighbourhood that is ingrained in your mind, the clothes that they hang across the roads, the plants they own.

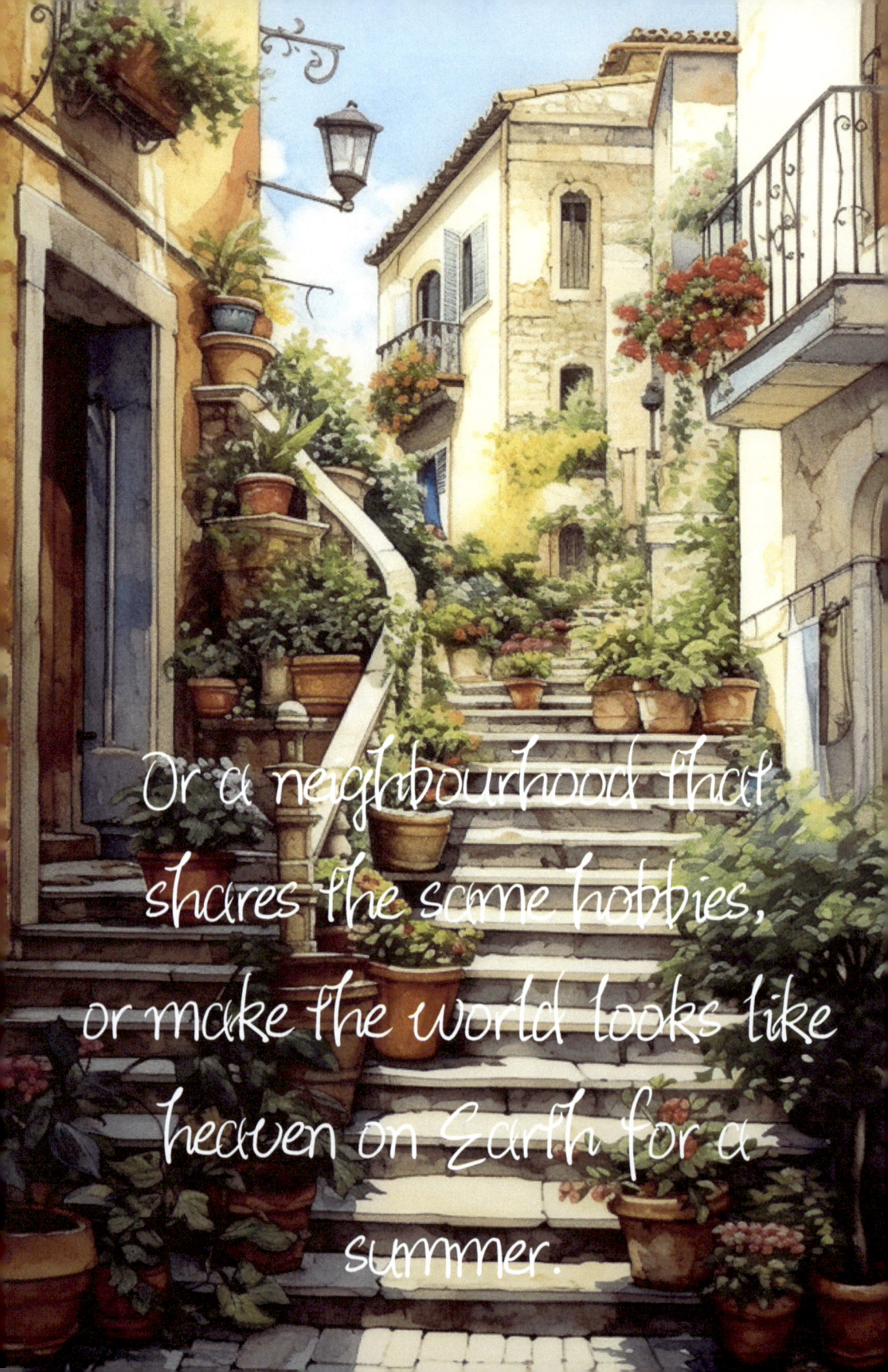

Or a neighbourhood that shares the same hobbies, or make the world looks like heaven on Earth for a summer.

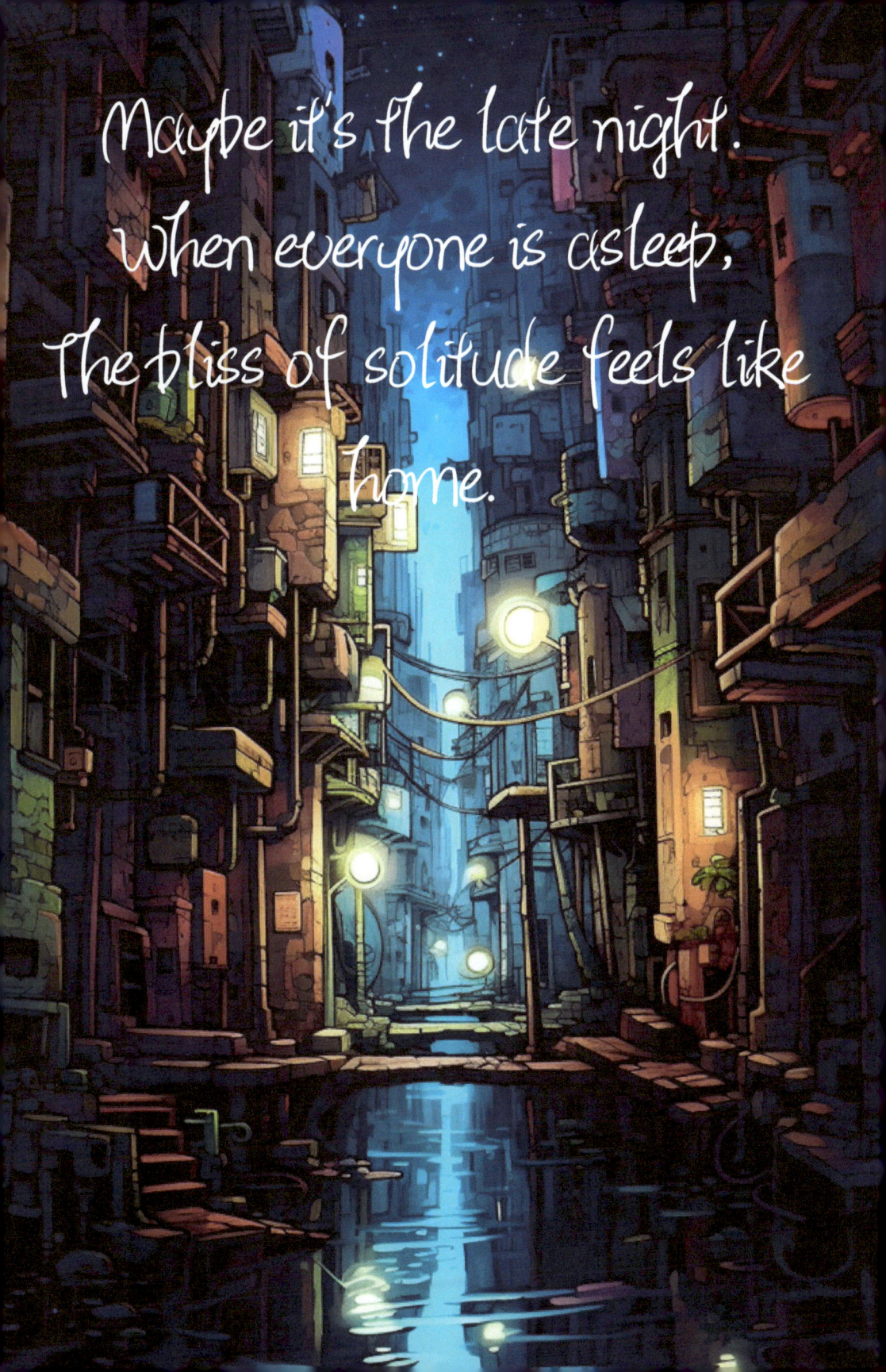

Maybe it's the late night. When everyone is asleep, The bliss of solitude feels like home.

Perhaps, the old hometown that you moved out decades ago. That's the Real Home.

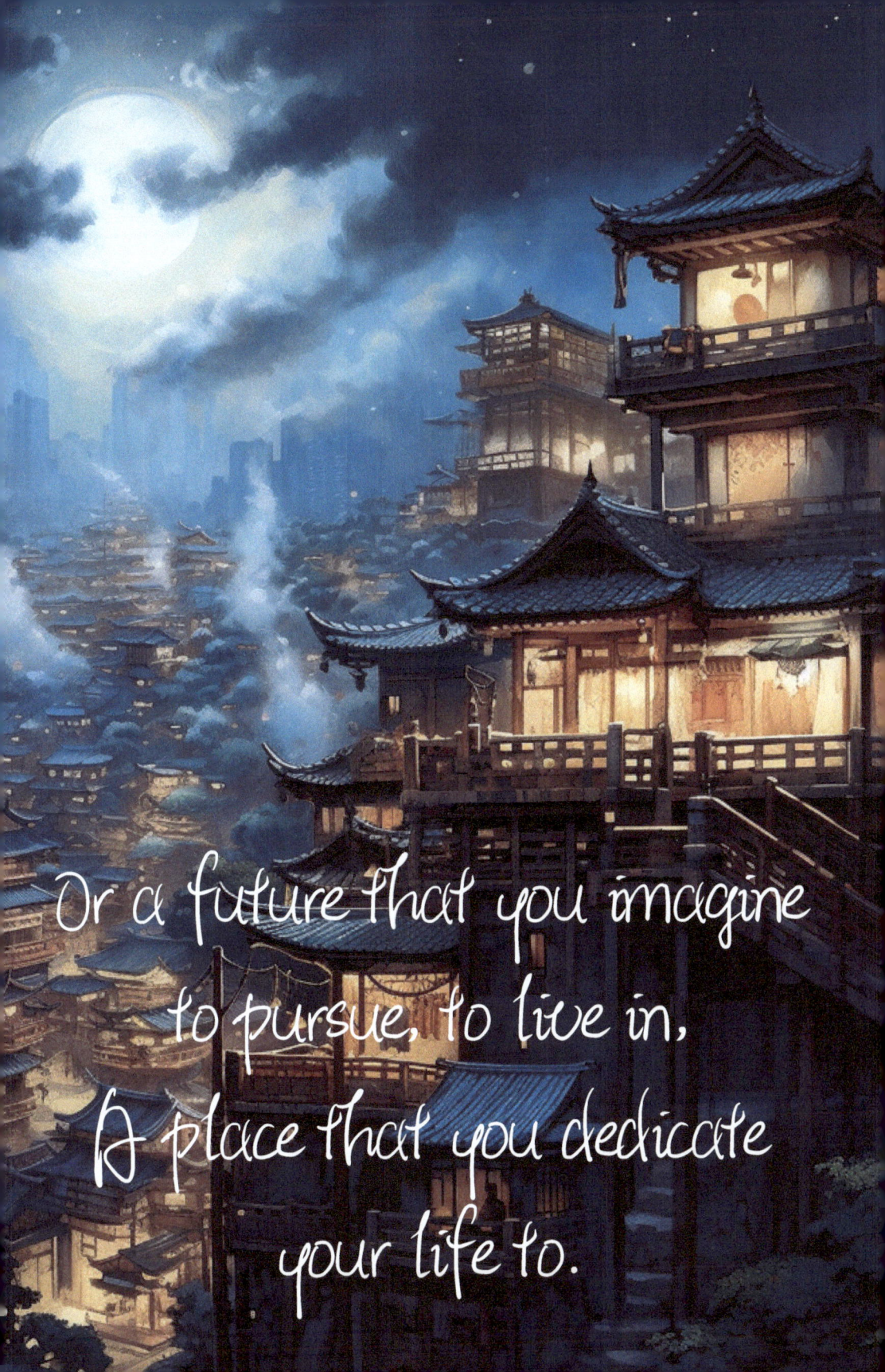

Or a future that you imagine to pursue, to live in, A place that you dedicate your life to.

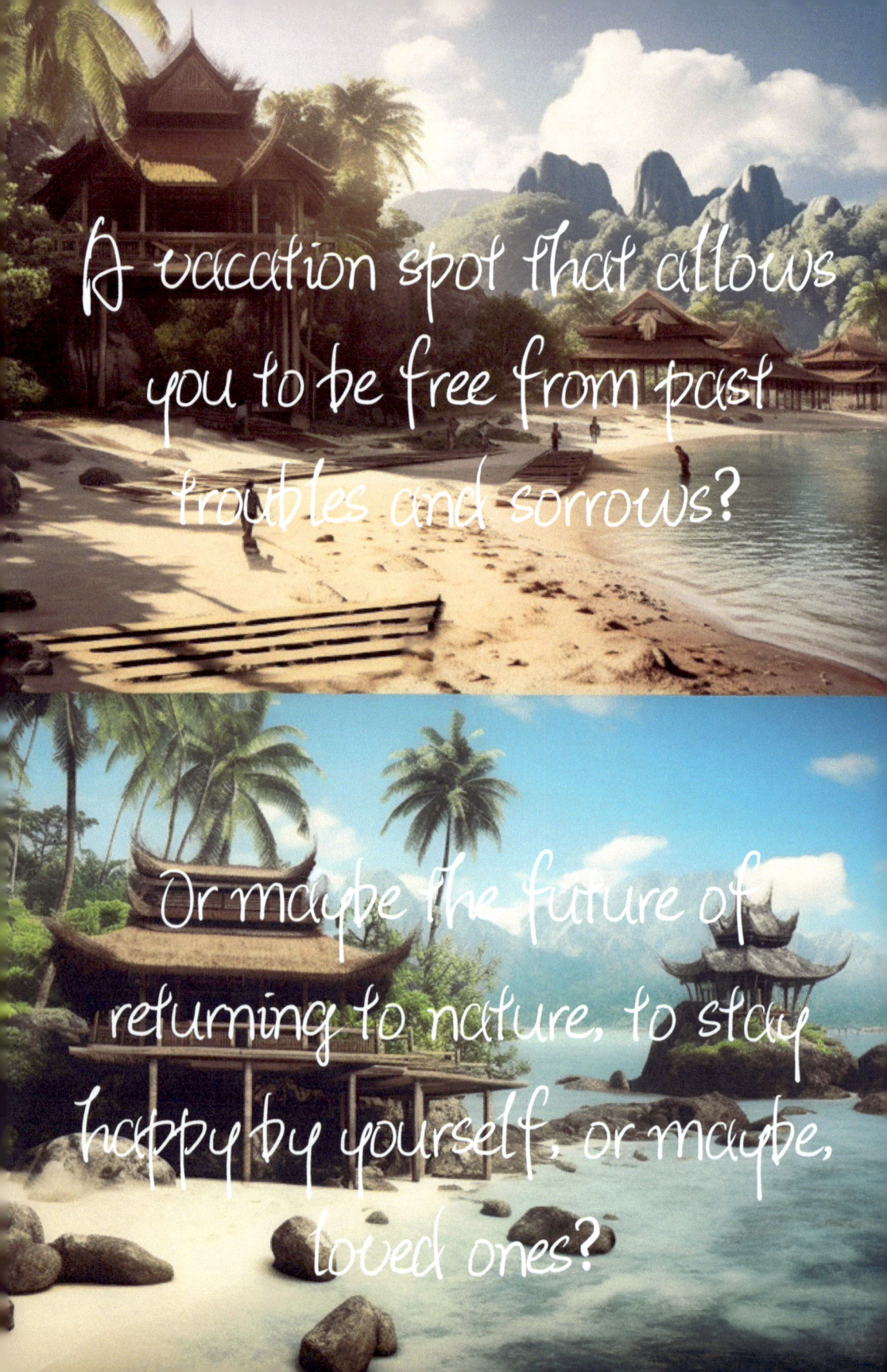

A vacation spot that allows you to be free from past troubles and sorrows?

Or maybe the future of returning to nature, to stay happy by yourself, or maybe, loved ones?

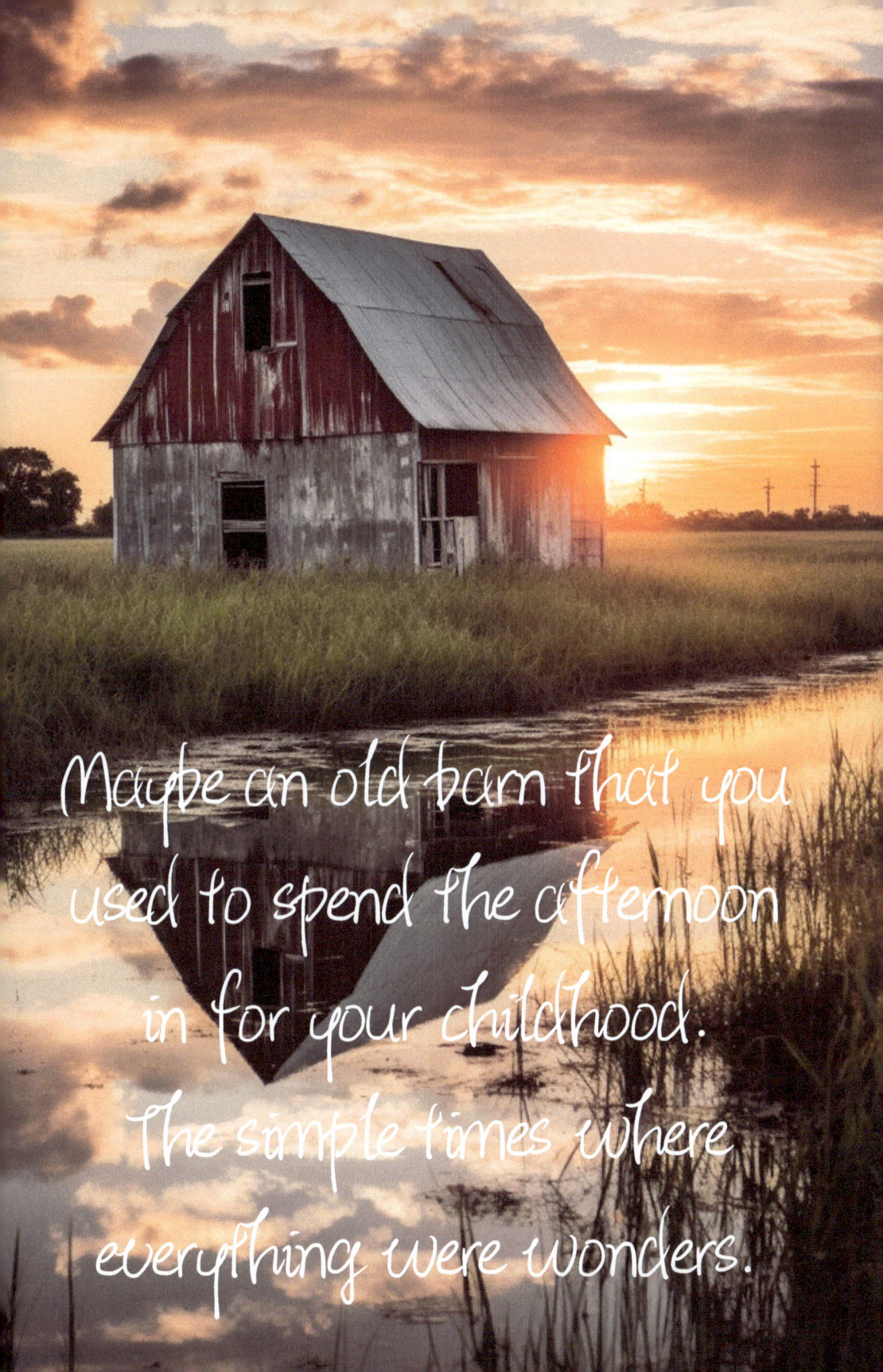

Maybe an old barn that you used to spend the afternoon in for your childhood. The simple times where everything were wonders.

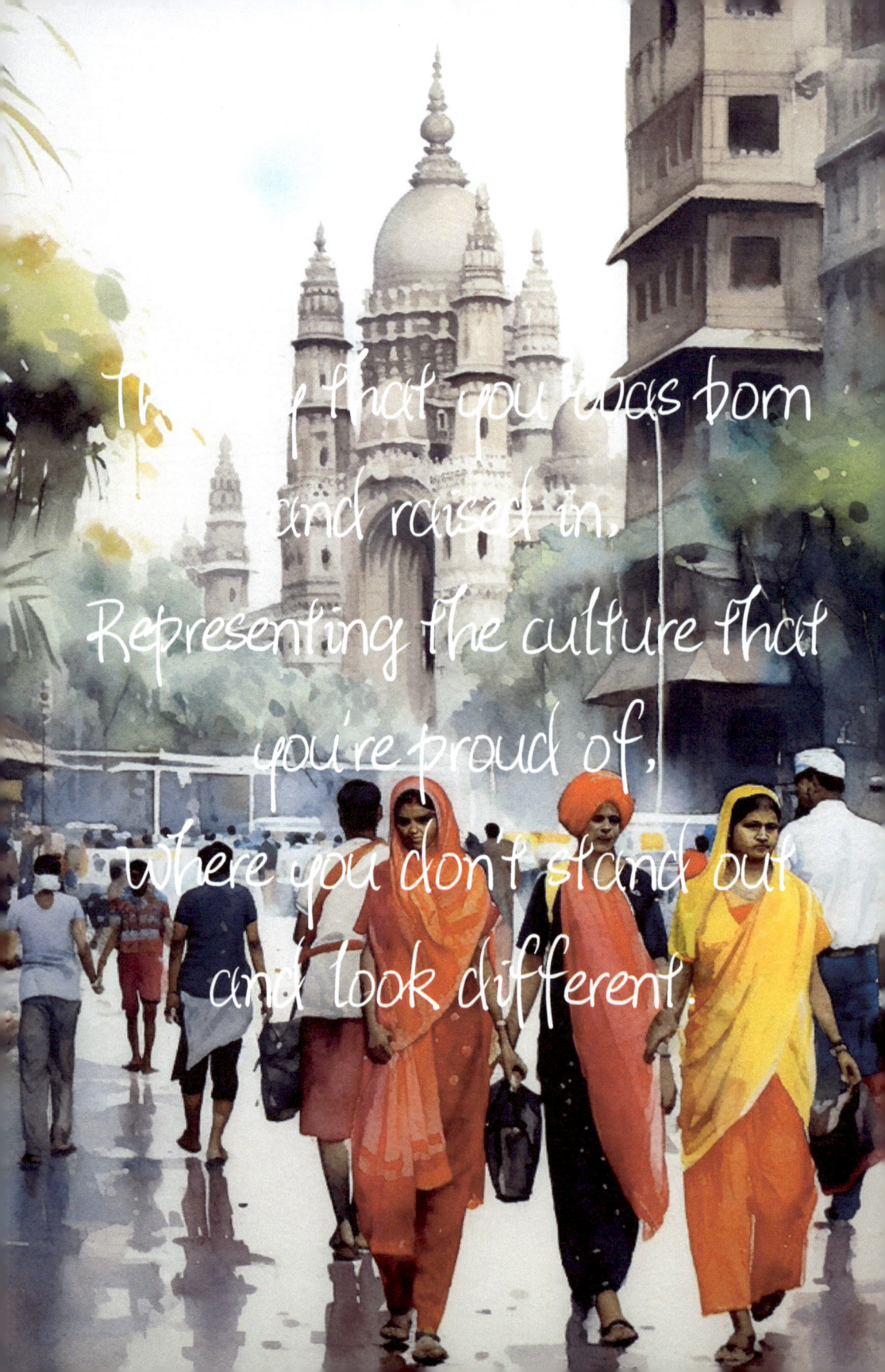

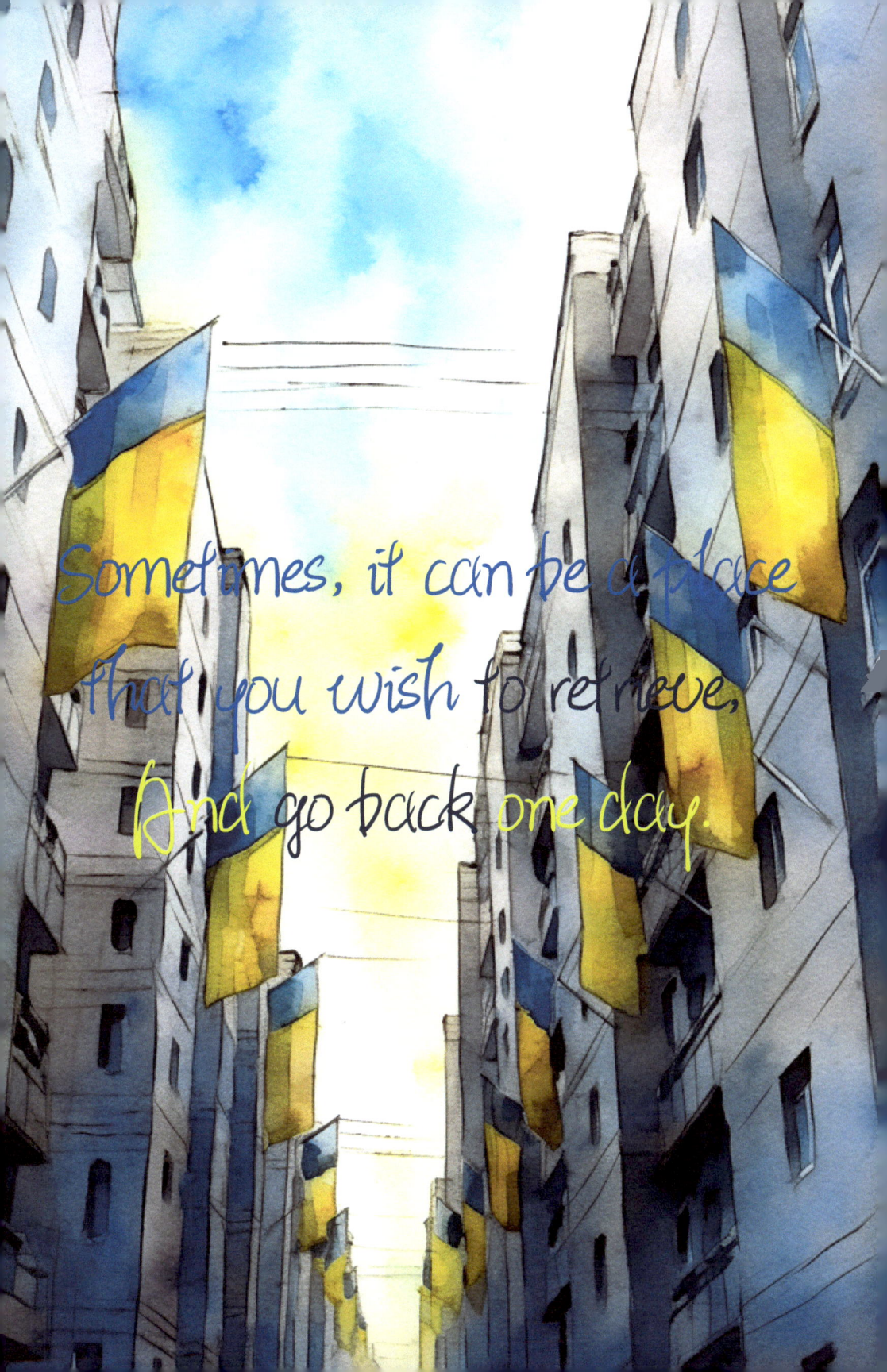

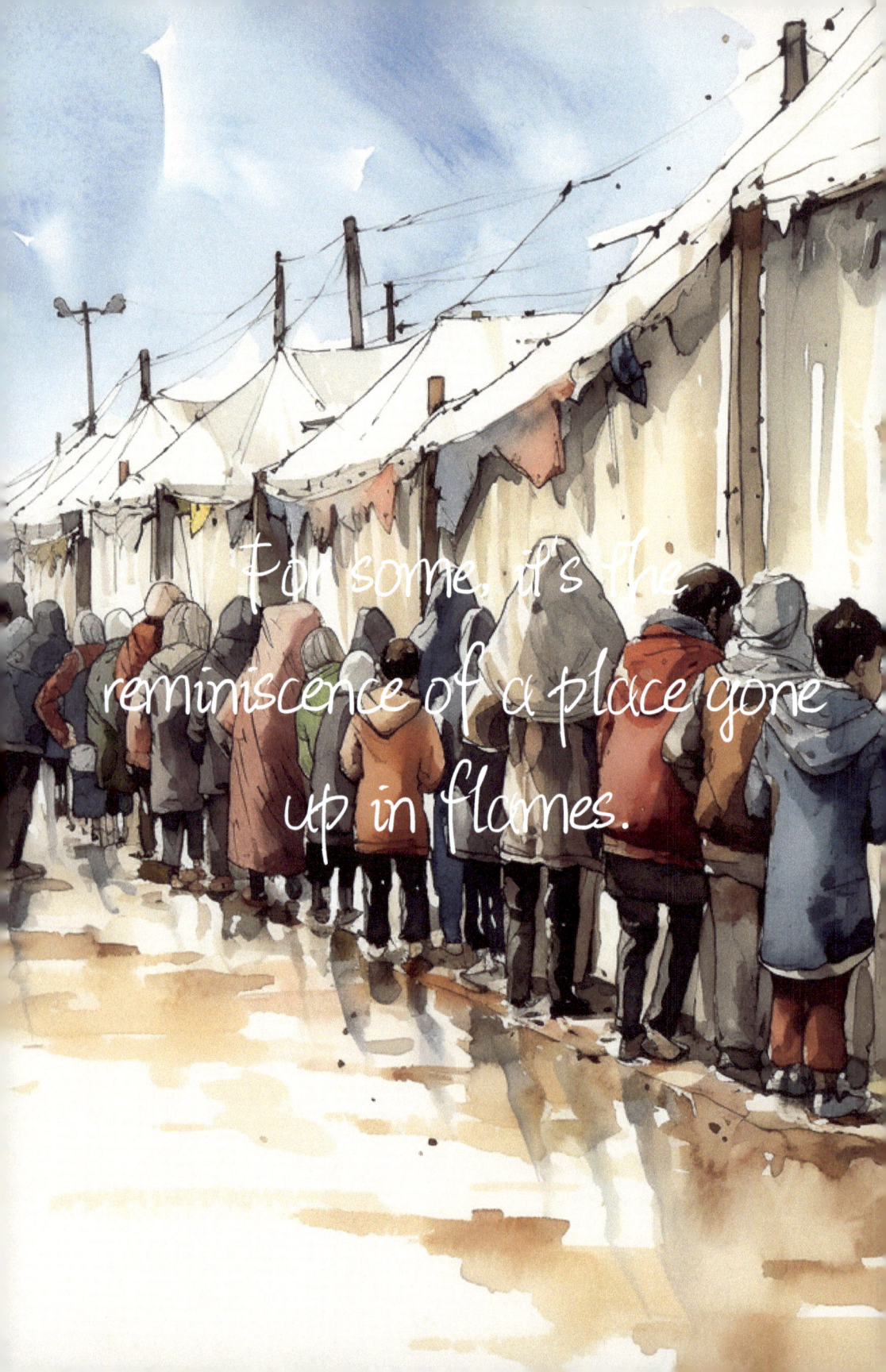

For some, it's the reminiscence of a place gone up in flames.

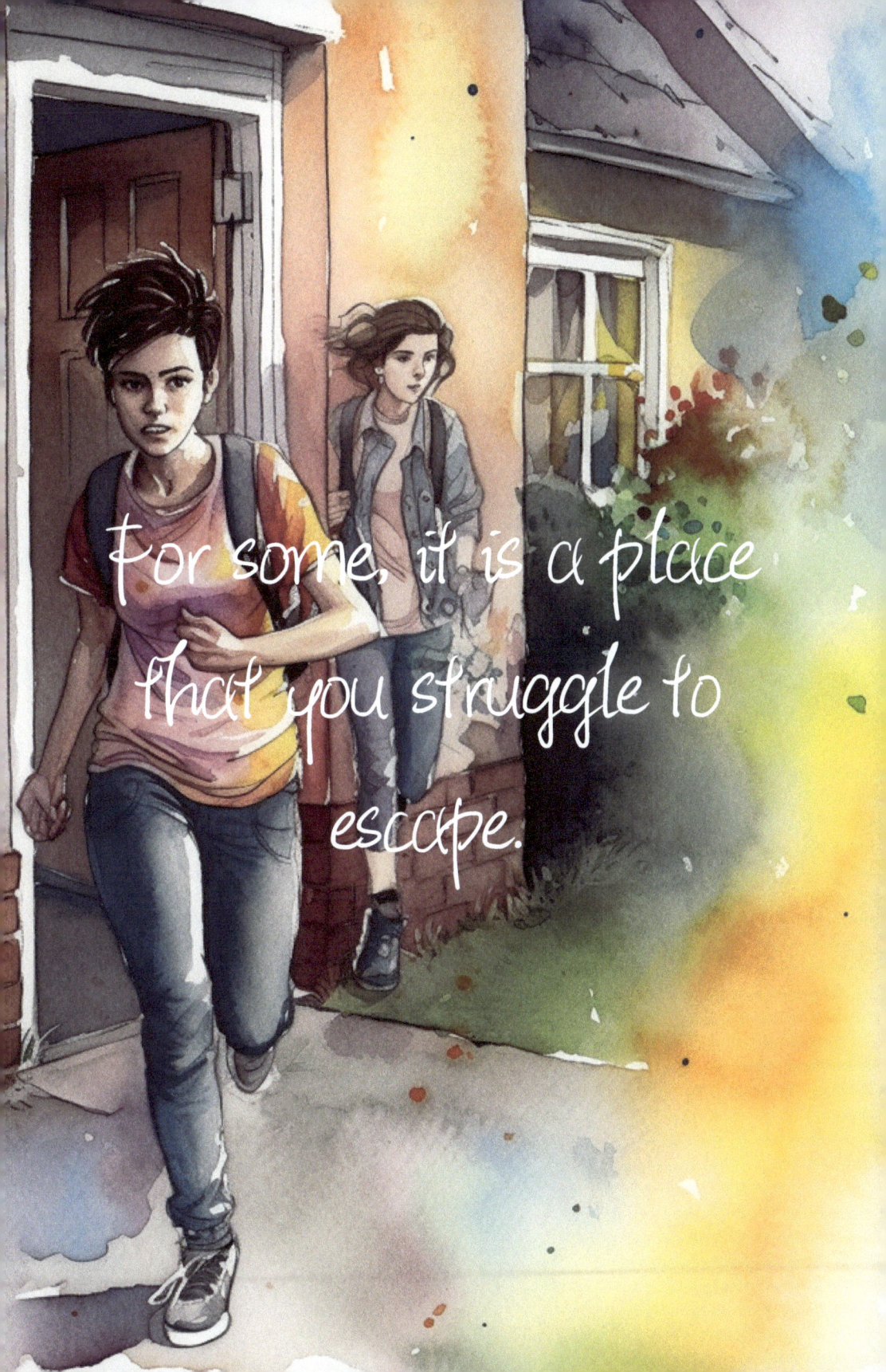

Some may find home a horror film with no men with superpowers or cape.

Home is supposedly to warm and safe, a cove to hide when the storms rage.

But some homes are broken,
full of regrets, and sadness.
A place that makes a step or
a knock on a door difficult.
Some homes are meant to
become mere memories,
fond or distasteful.

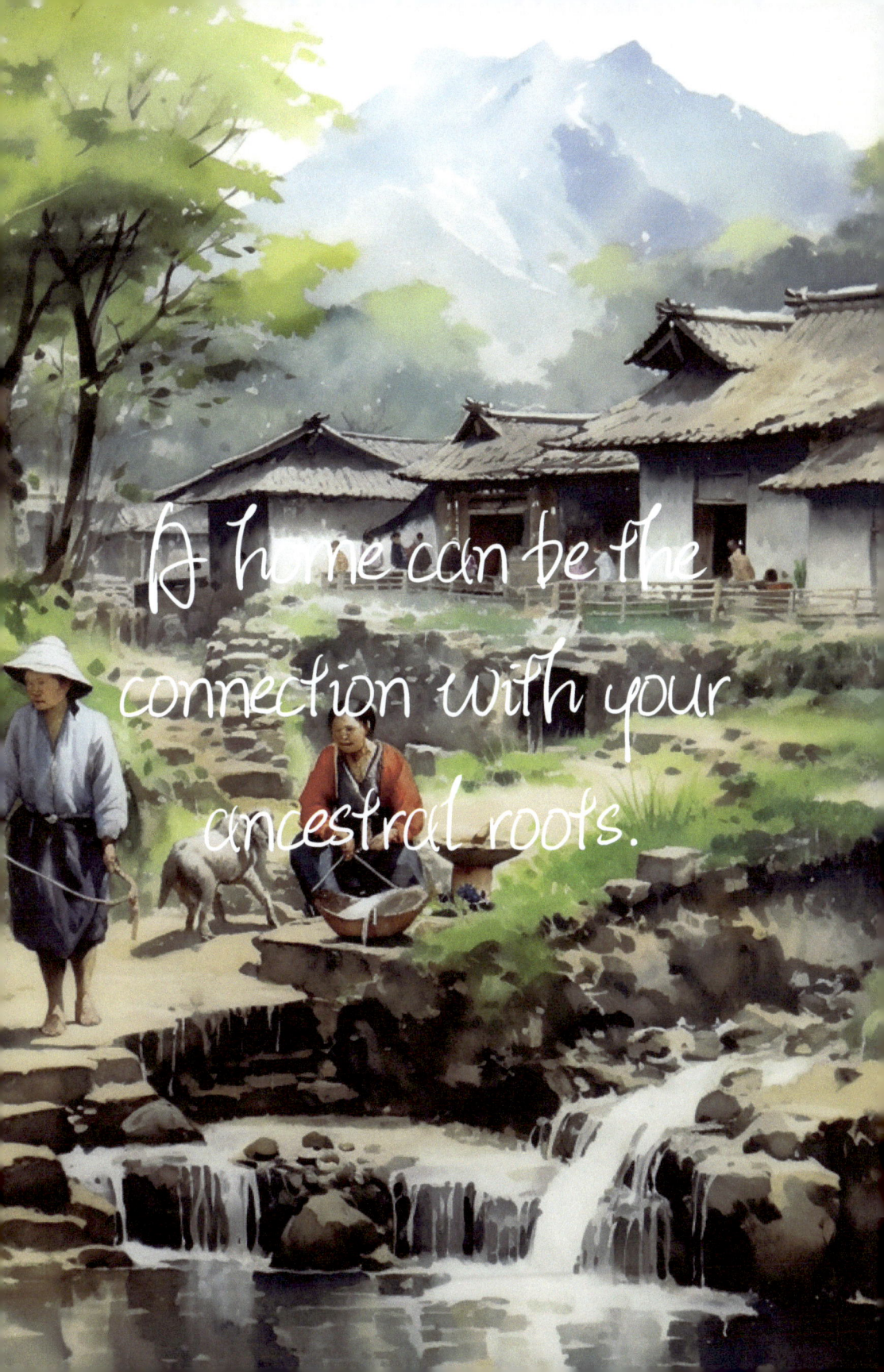

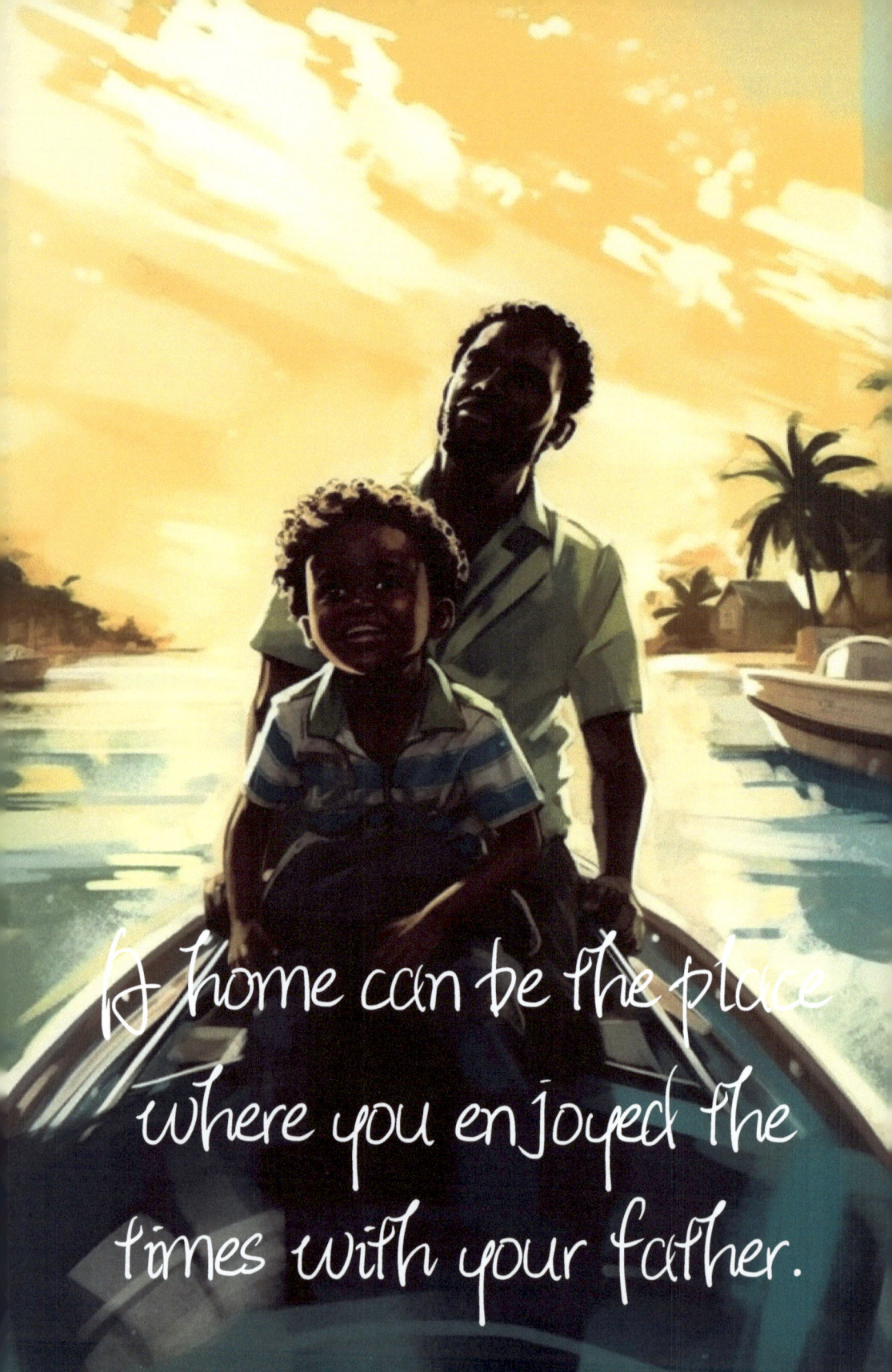

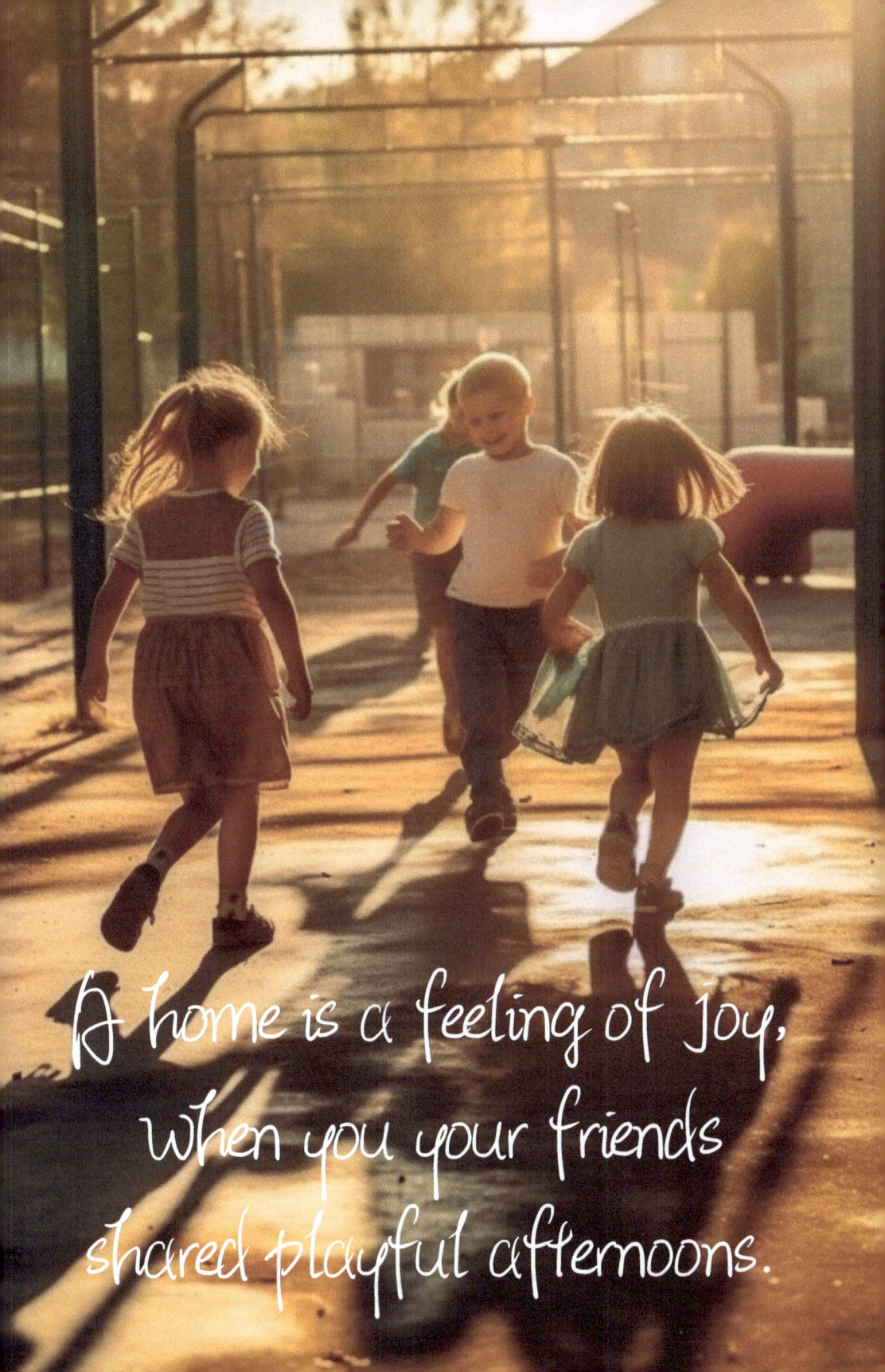
A home is a feeling of joy, when you your friends shared playful afternoons.

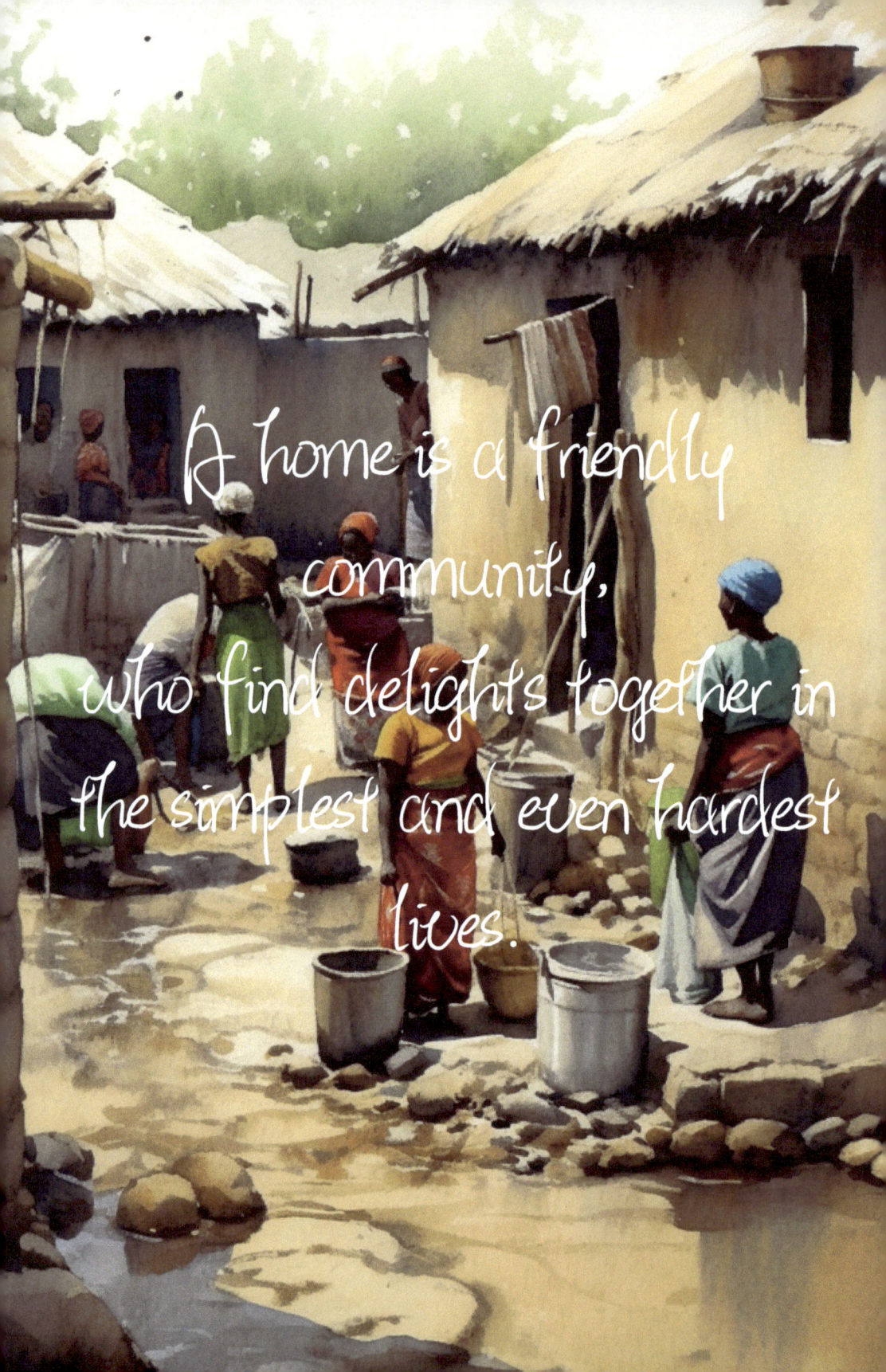

A home is a friendly community, who find delights together in the simplest and even hardest lives.

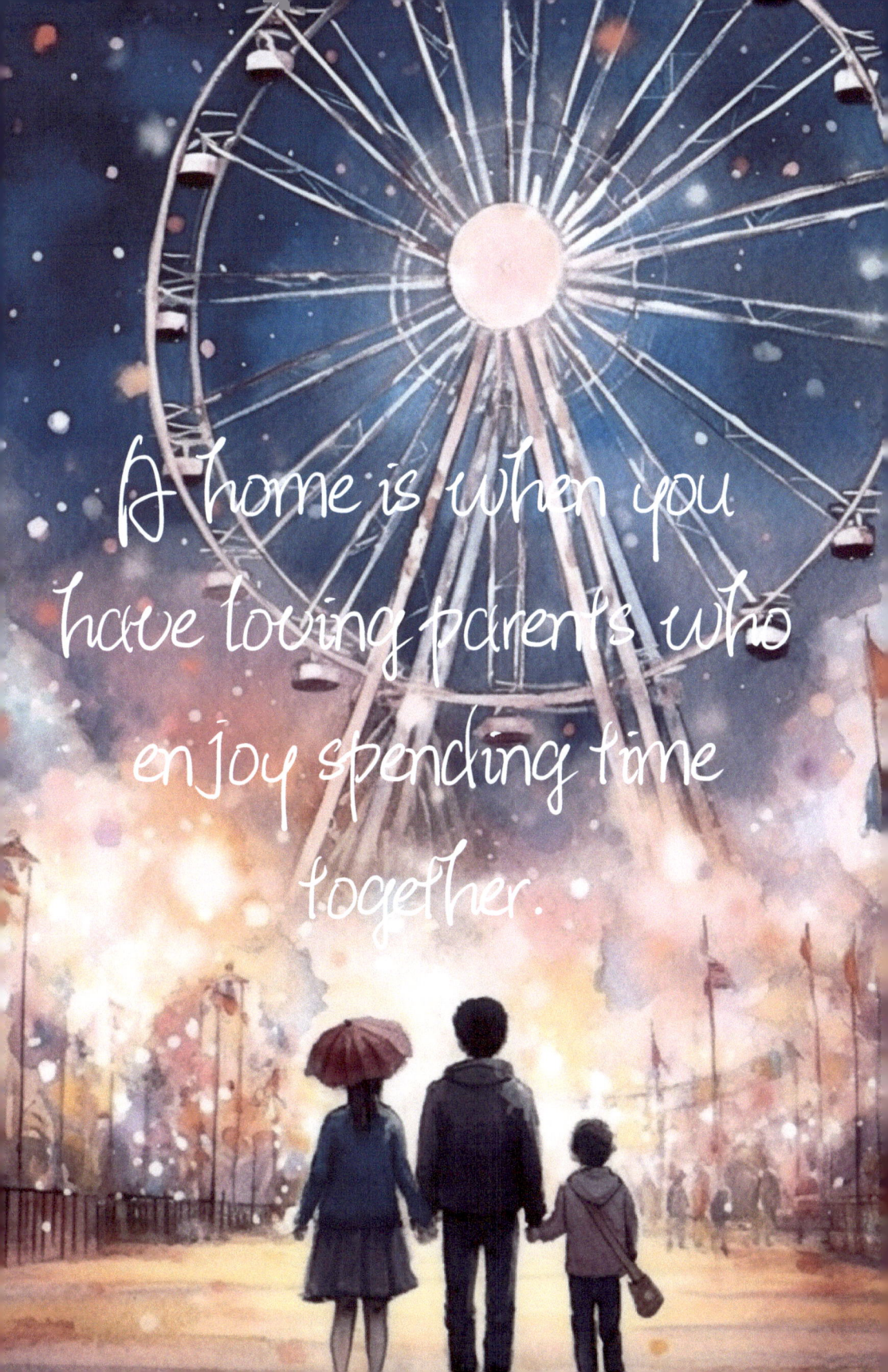

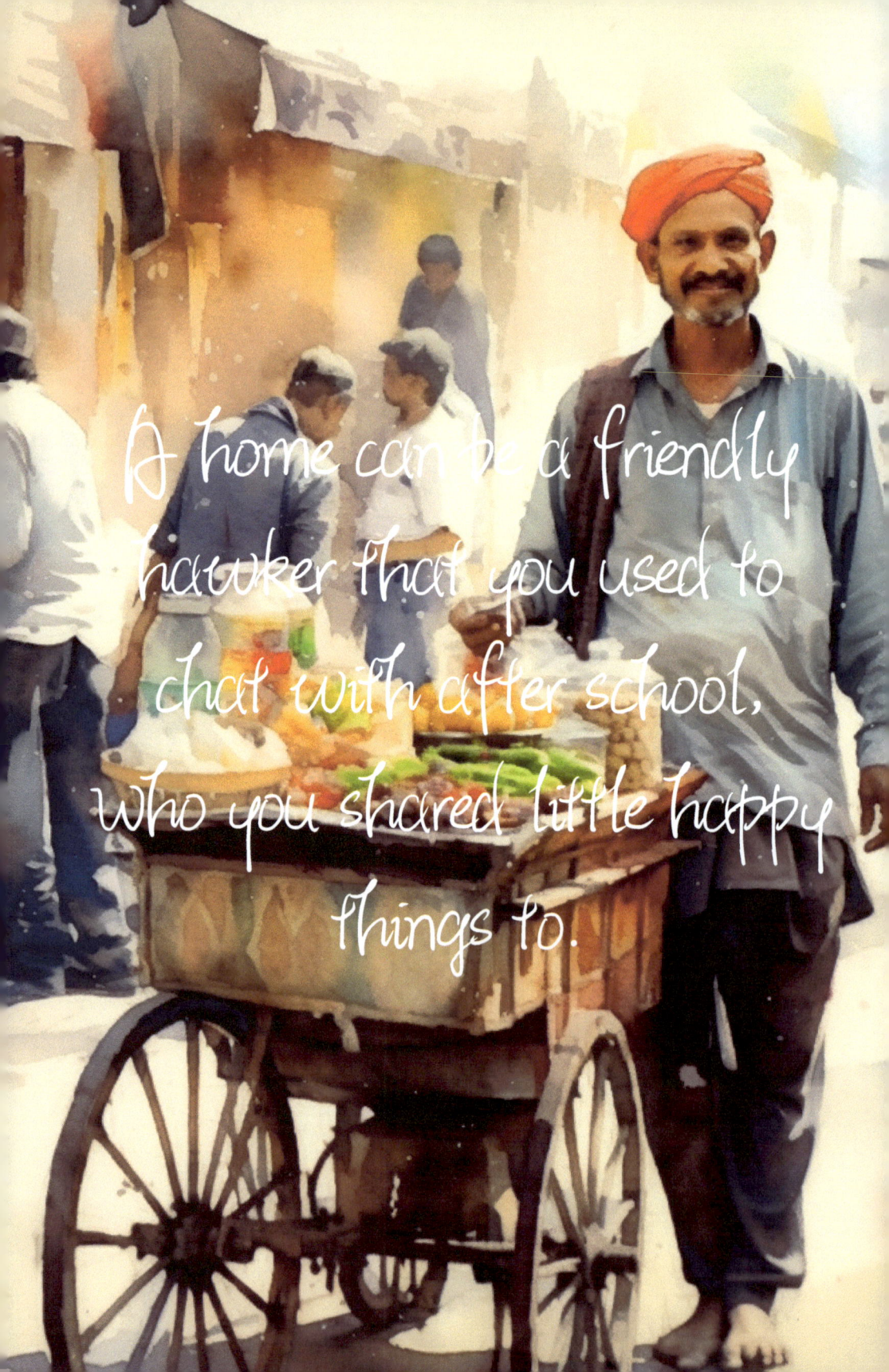

A home can be the time with your grandparents, when they taught you everything they've learnt, passion and love sparkled in their eyes.

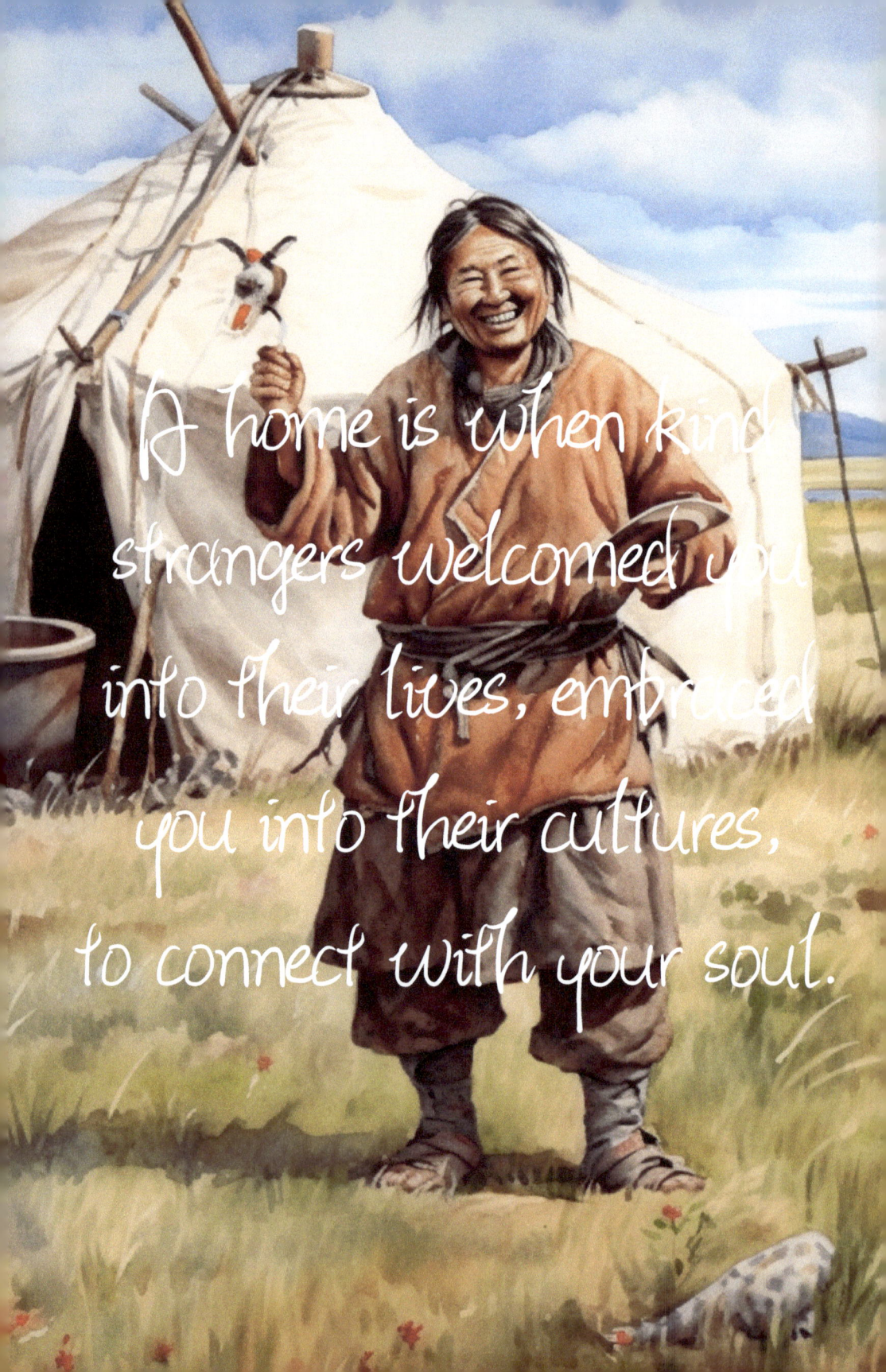

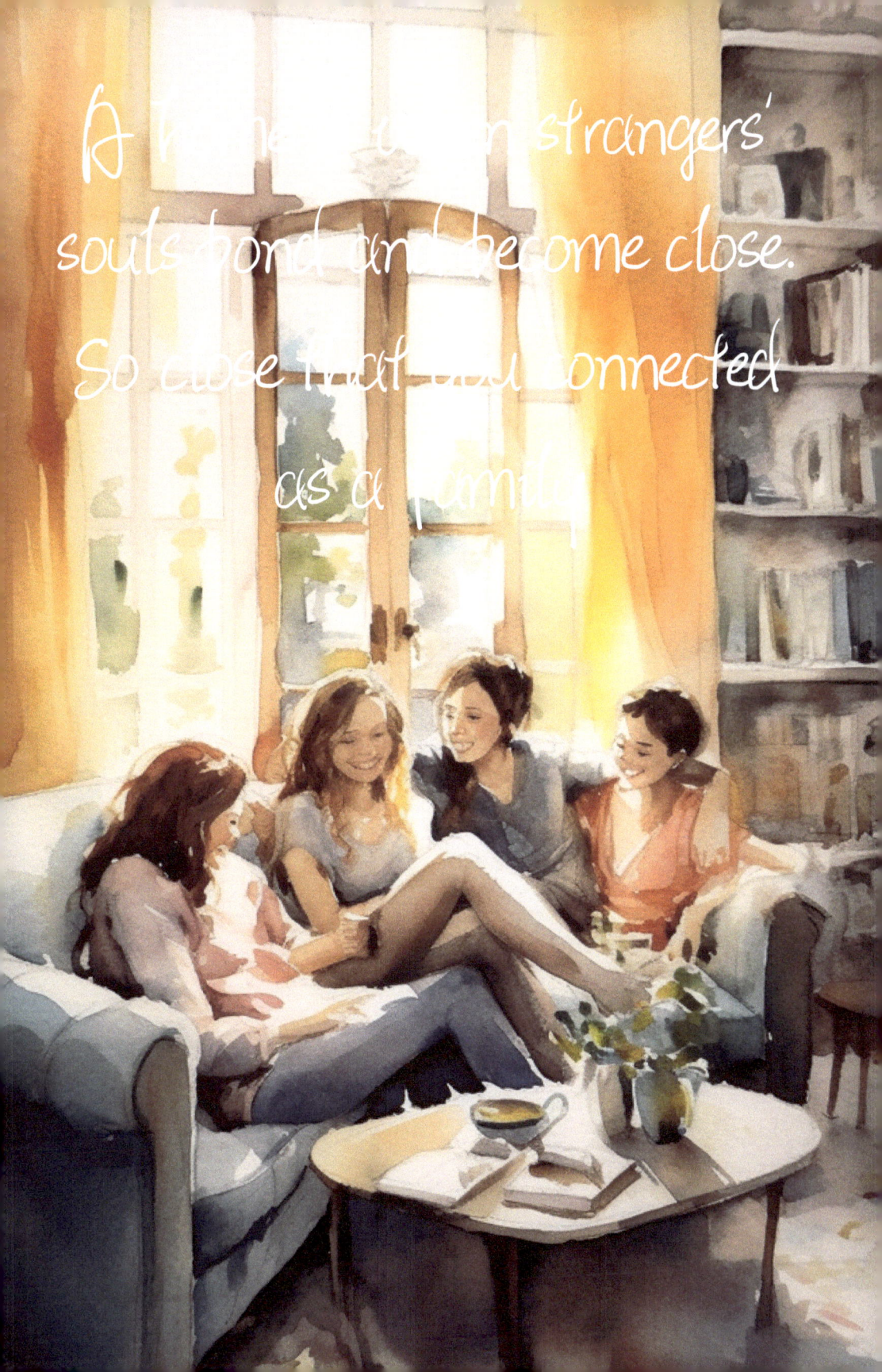

A home where strangers'
souls bond and become close.
So close that also connected
as a family.

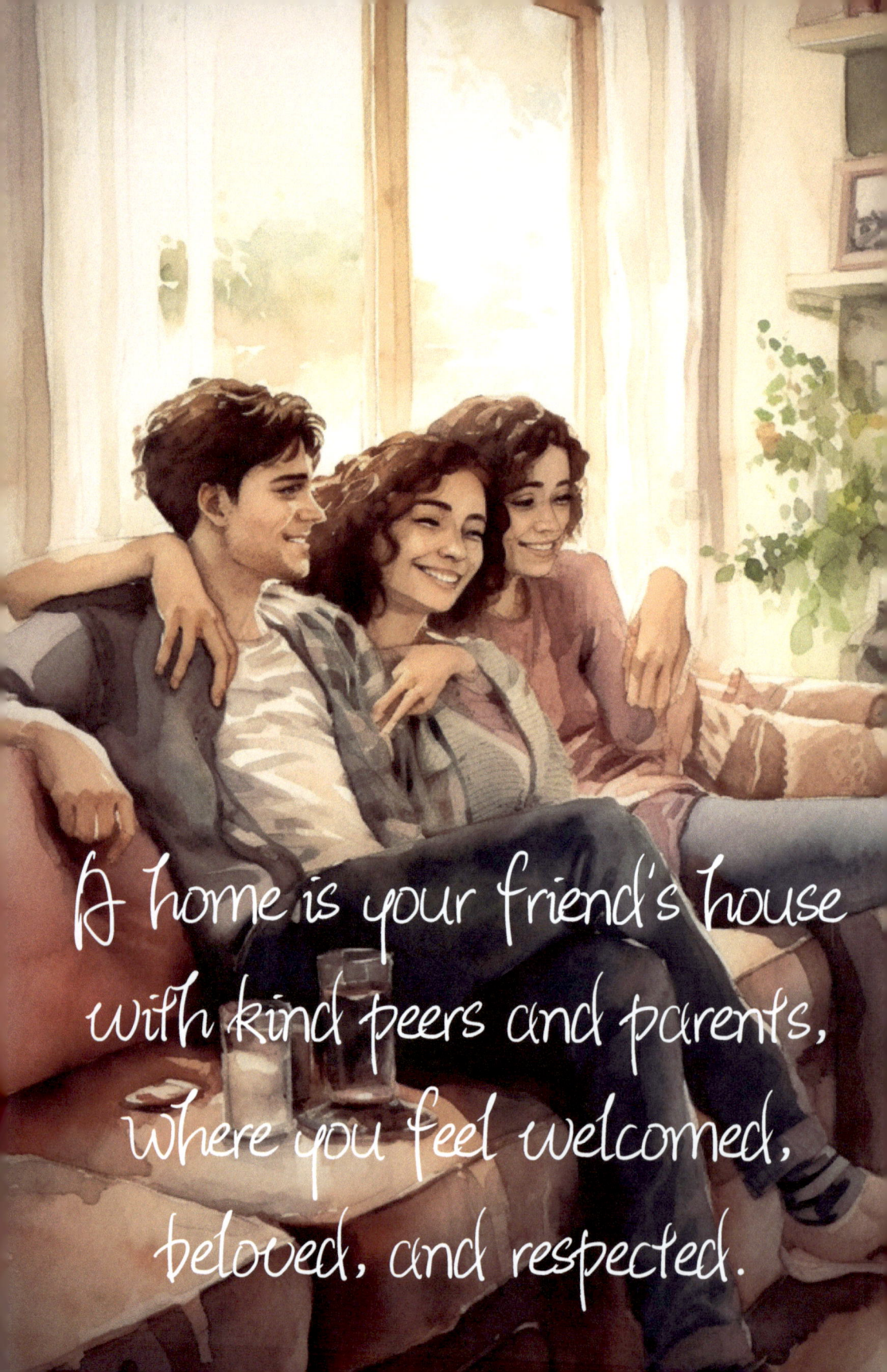

A home is a group that can laugh together, cry together, And be one another's comfort.

A home is the times to share the same passion, dedicate your lives onto the same dream, with people you love.

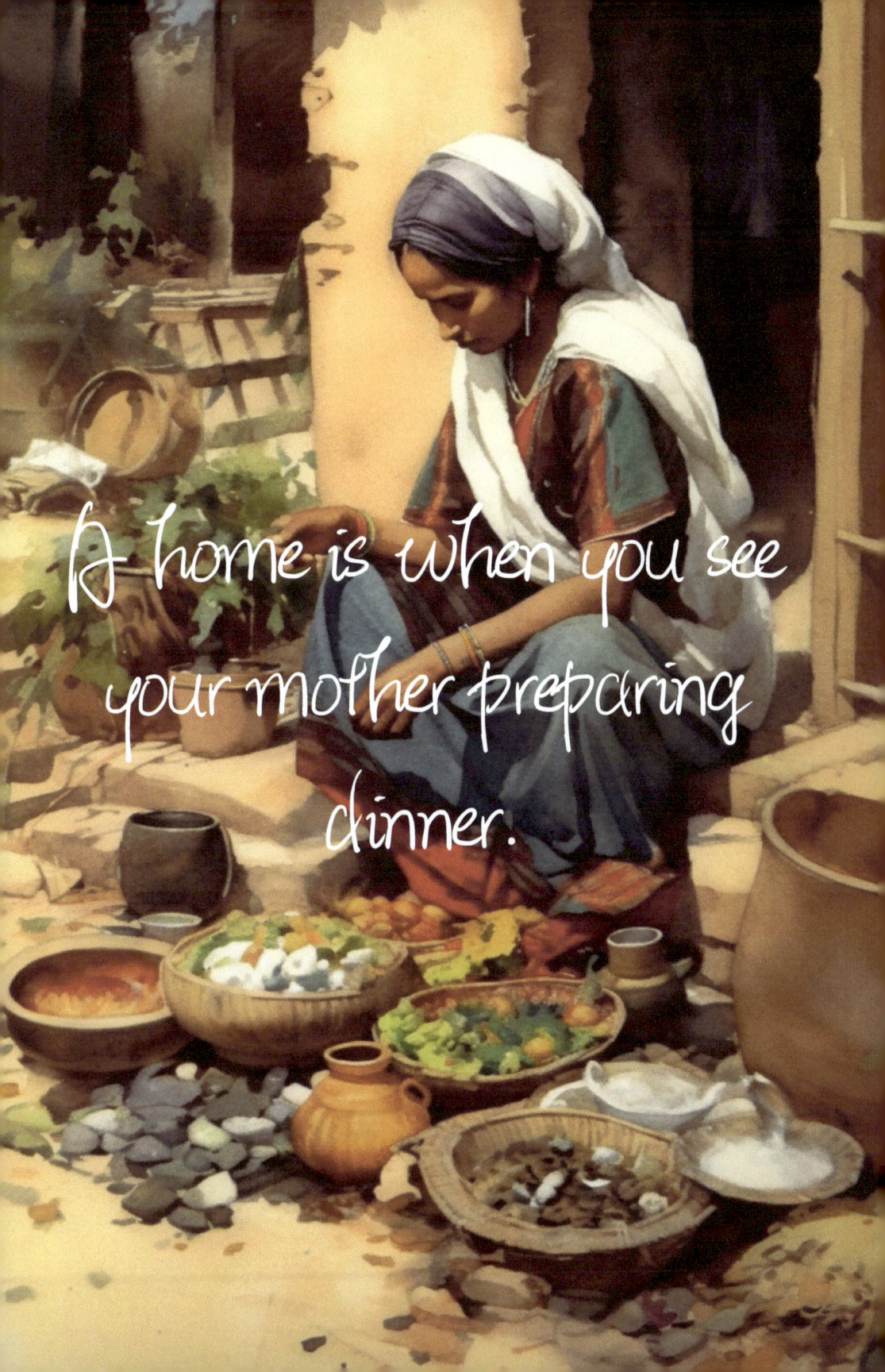

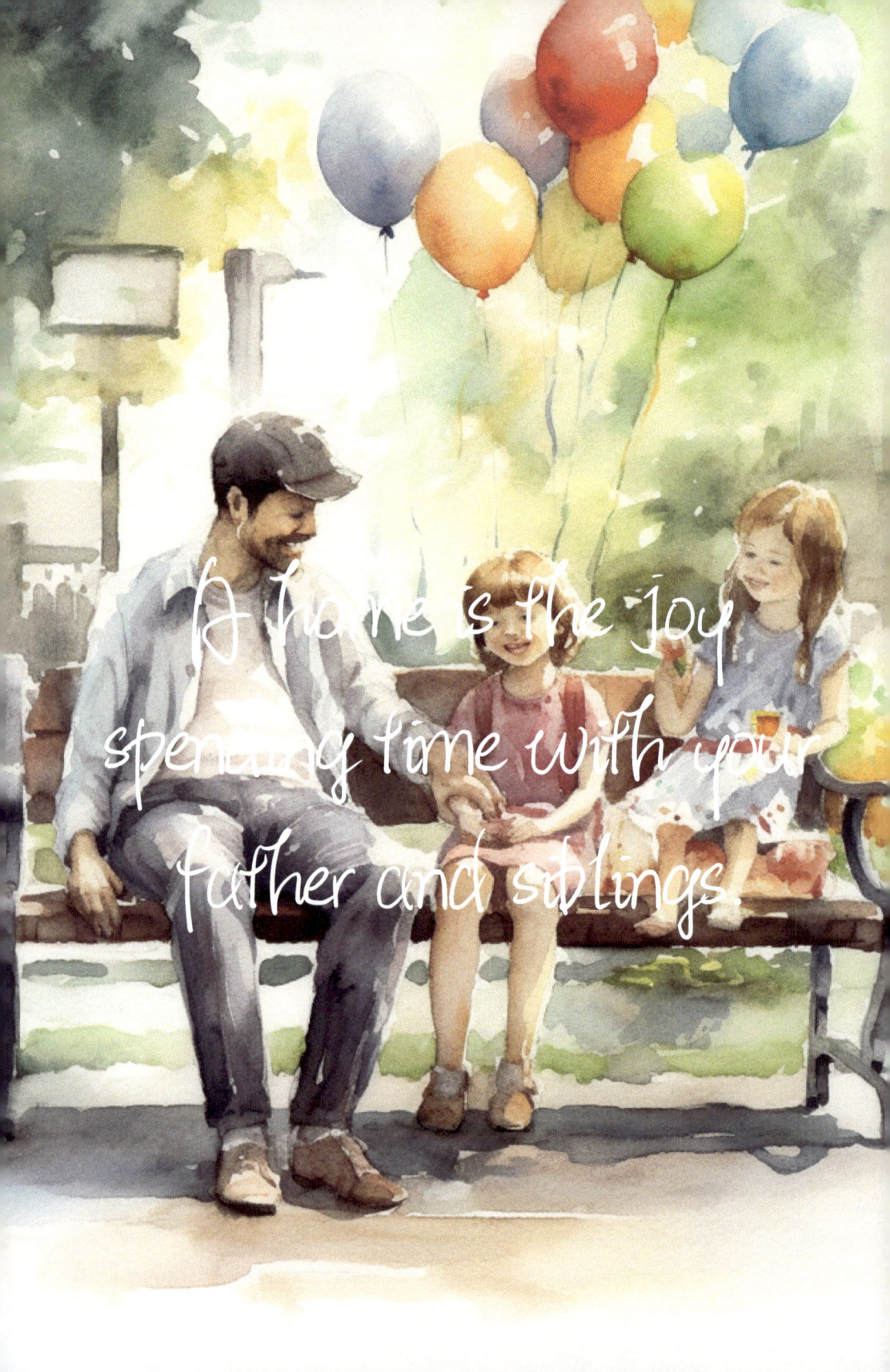

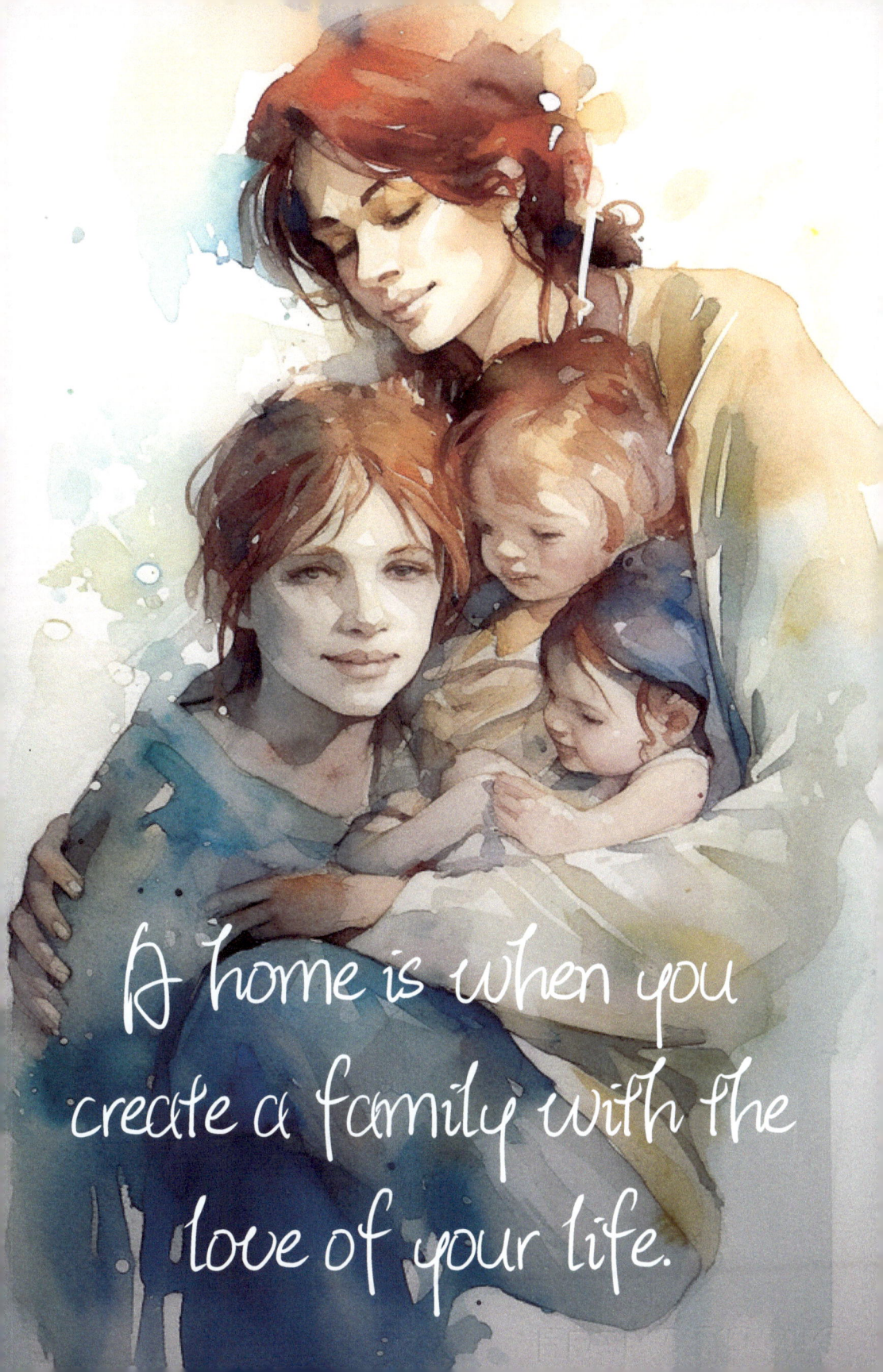

*Some may have two homes,
And that's alright.
As long as there is love,
There is home.*

Some find the sea is the embracing home they love and long for.

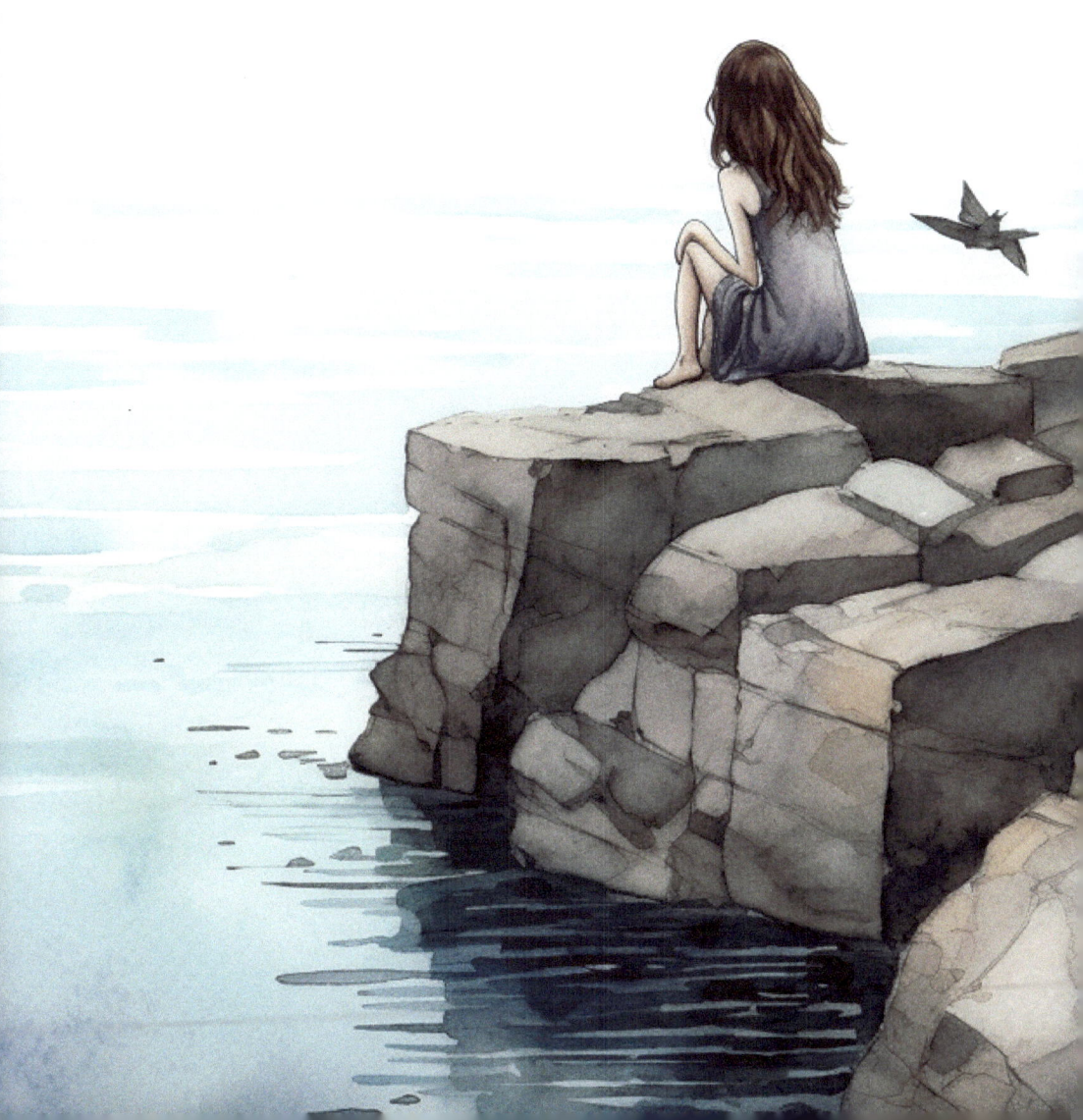

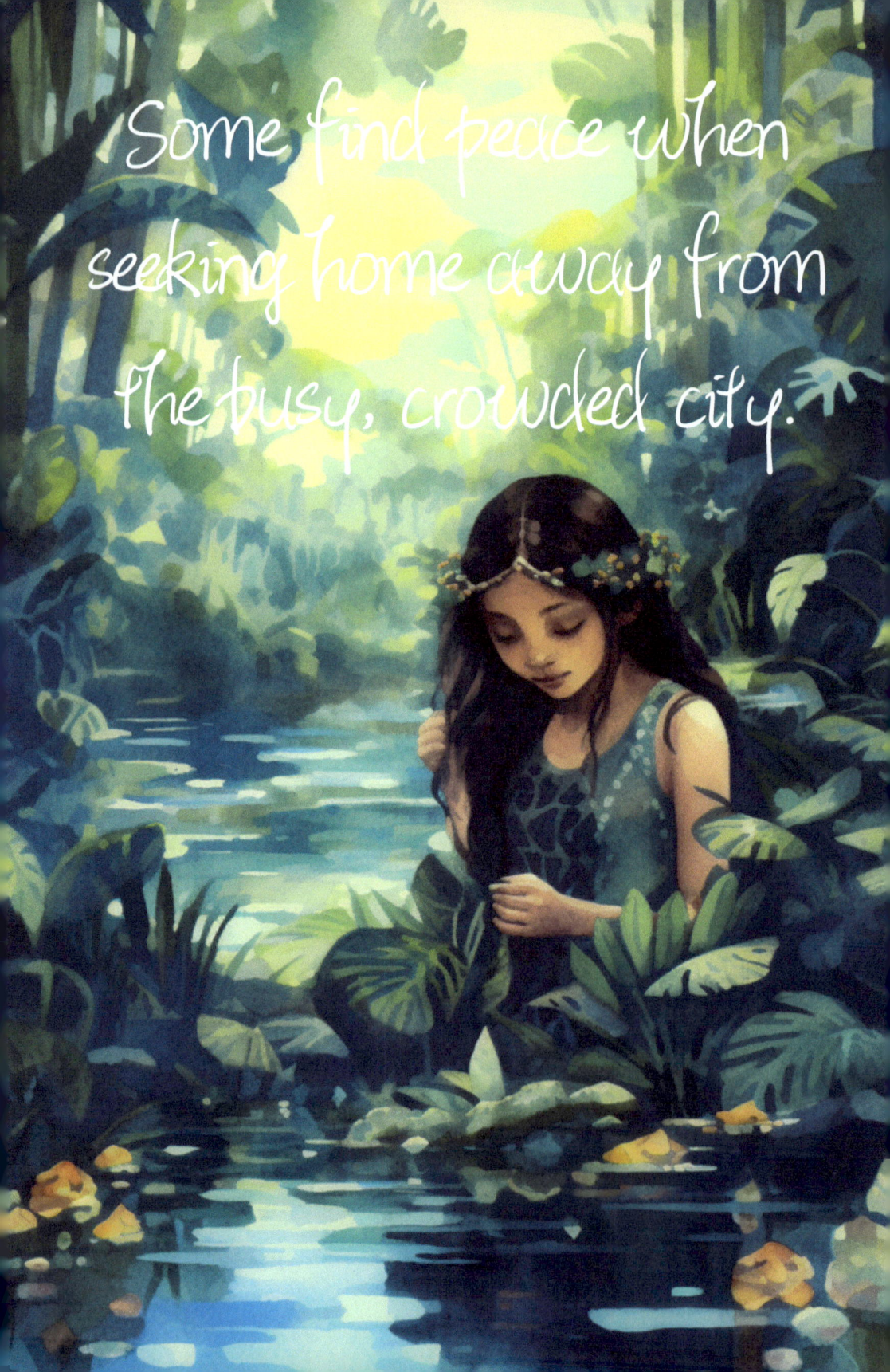

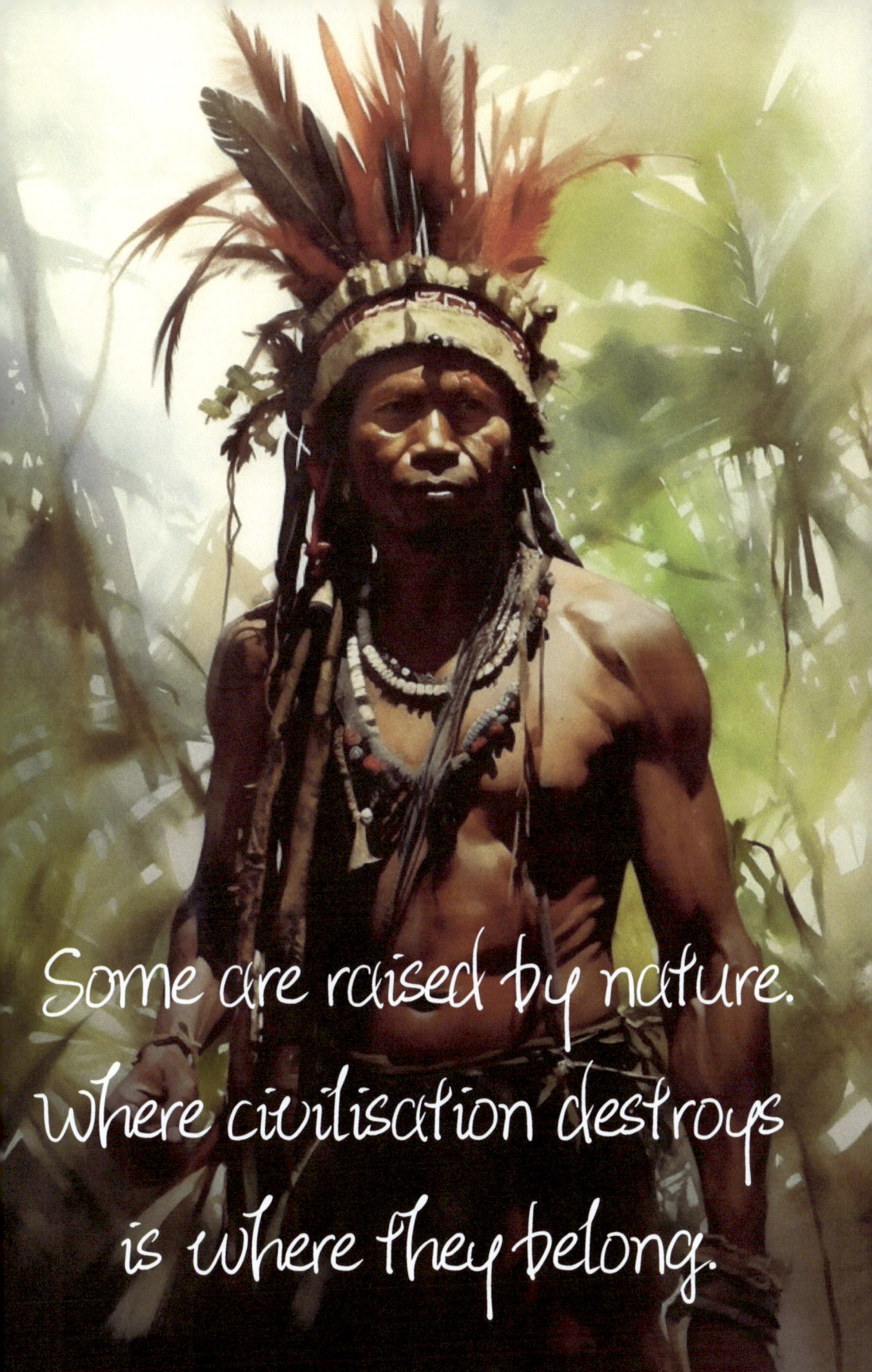

A home can be a life that you're content. Alone but never lonely.

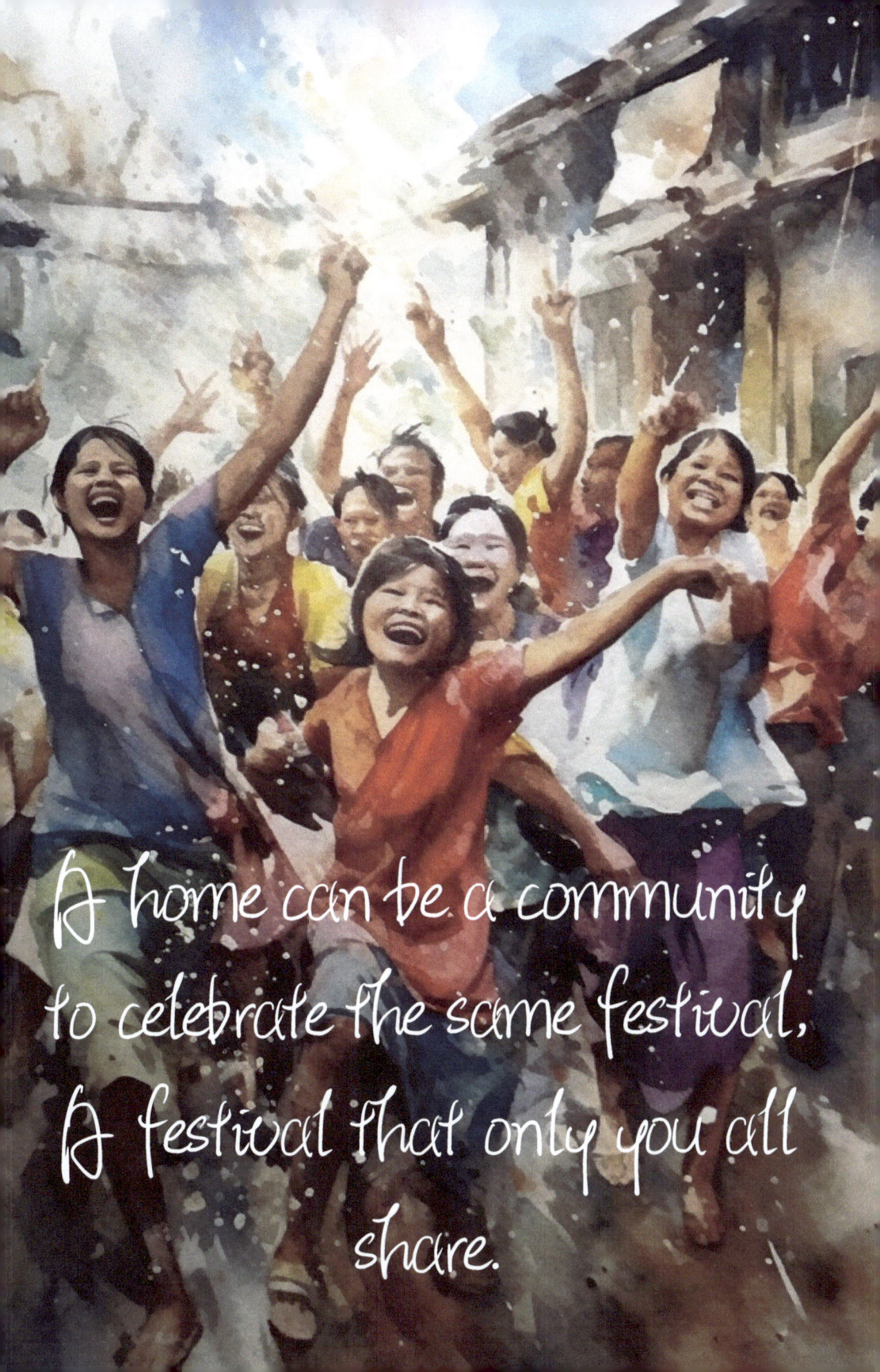

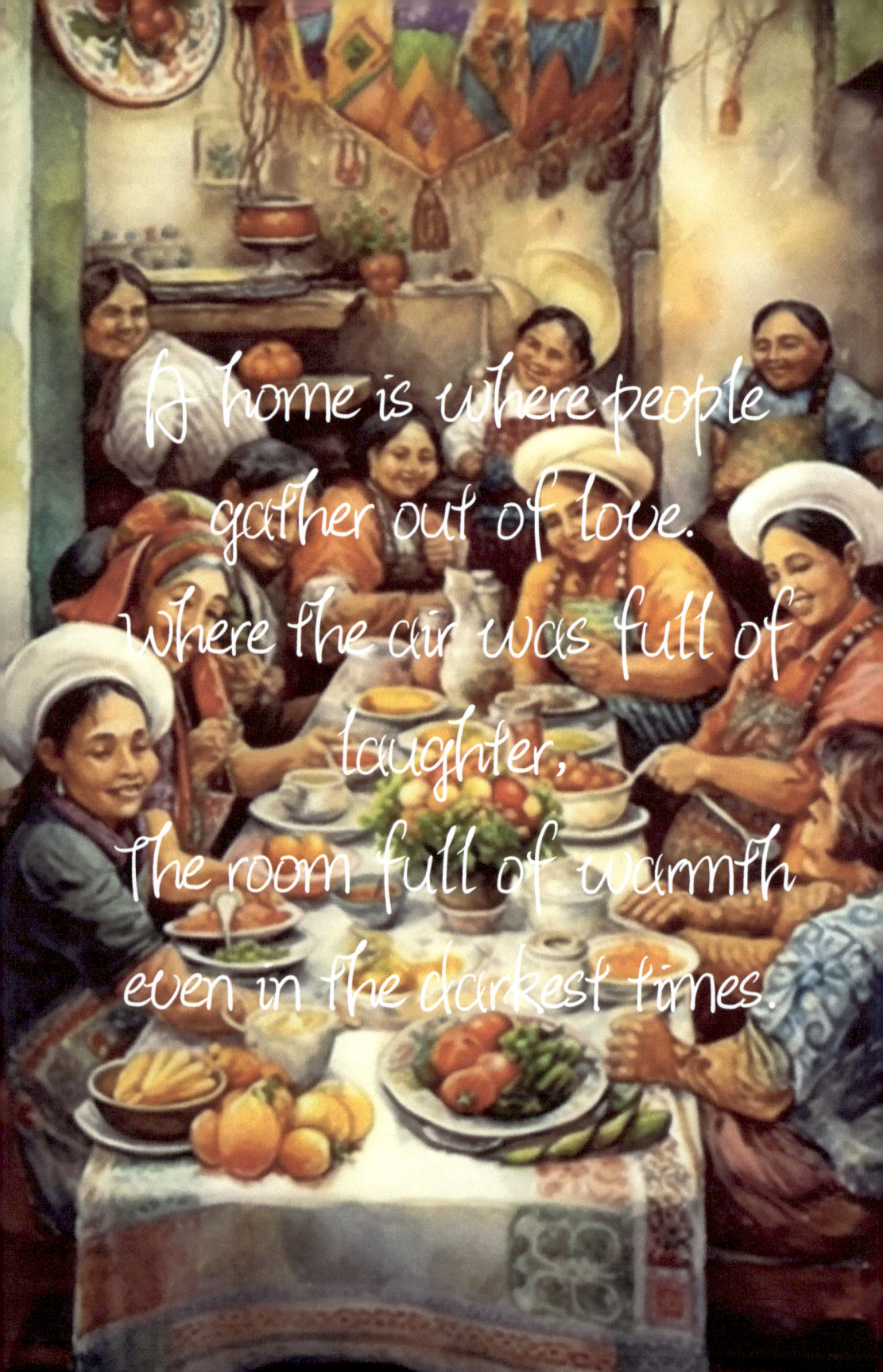

A home is where children can be safe and happy, taken care of and blessed by kind guardians.

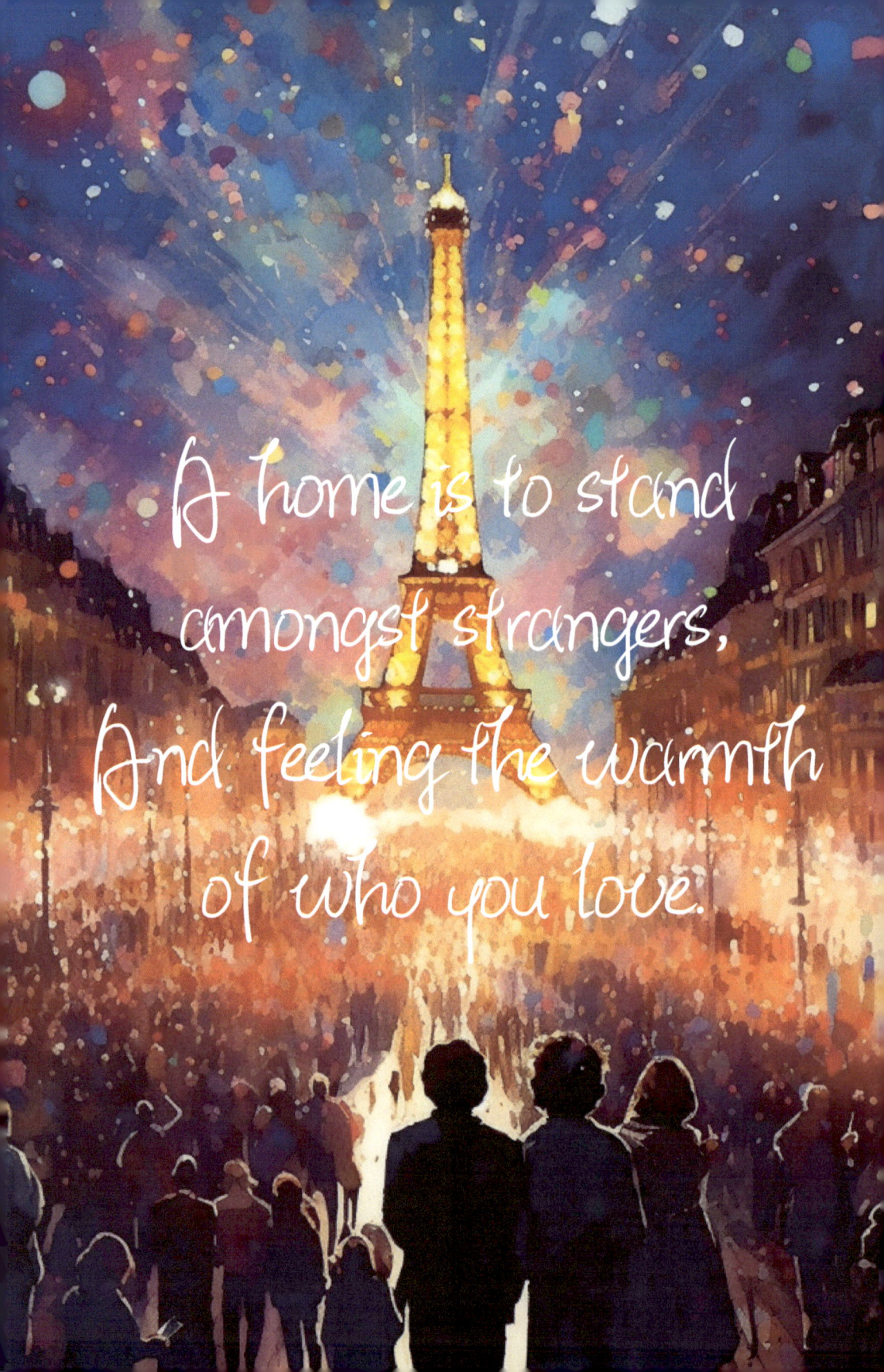

A home is a place,
Where loving memories
were made.
Where people remind you
of the worth of life,
And show you where
happiness hides.

A home is where souls connect
and bond,
Where the love and warmth of
the world rush in your mind,
That you feel vulnerable but
empowered,
Distant from the world's
horror,
And close to the world's gifts.

A home is where you are happy and safe. Where you can be yourself and see yourself. Where you can be alone but never lonely.

All souls deserve a real
home,
Where their lights can shine
with no fear,
Where they can bond with no
shame.
When all the souls can feel
the same,
The world becomes everyone's
home.